Putting Learning Before Technology!

For many, digitalization is the key to revolutionizing education. But what do we know about its impact on the learning process? What benefits are on offer and what are the risks? What are the consequences for educational interventions?

Putting Learning Before Technology! discusses these questions and more in a thorough exploration of the use of technology in educational settings. Central to the author's argument is that digitalization as a sole and structural measure will bring little benefit and that the teachers who bring lessons to life are much more important. Features of the book include:

- evidence from Visible Learning research to scientifically frame the effectiveness and pitfalls of technology in the classroom;
- real-life classroom examples;
- graphics to clearly illustrate key concepts and studies.

This book is a fascinating analysis of the impact, possibilities, and limits of the use of technology within education, and will appeal to teachers and teacher-trainers in any setting or country.

Klaus Zierer is Professor of Education at the University of Augsburg, Germany, and Associate Research Fellow of the ESRC-funded Centre on Skills, Knowledge and Organisational Performance (SKOPE) at the University of Oxford, UK. He is co-author with John Hattie of the recently published *10 Mindframes for Visible Learning*.

T0398125

Putting Learning Before Technology!

The Possibilities and Limits of Digitalization

Klaus Zierer

Routledge
Taylor & Francis Group

LONDON AND NEW YORK

First published 2019
by Routledge
2 Park Square, Milton Park, Abingdon, Oxon OX14 4RN

and by Routledge
52 Vanderbilt Avenue, New York, NY 10017

Routledge is an imprint of the Taylor & Francis Group, an informa business

© 2019 Klaus Zierer

British Library Cataloguing-in-Publication Data
A catalogue record for this book is available from the British Library

Library of Congress Cataloging-in-Publication Data
Names: Zierer, Klaus, author.
Title: Putting learning before technology! : the possibilities and limits of digitalization / Klaus Zierer.
Description: Abingdon, Oxon ; New York, NY : Routledge, 2019. | Includes bibliographical references and index.
Identifiers: LCCN 2018043344 | ISBN 9781138320505 (hbk) | ISBN 9781138320512 (pbk) | ISBN 9780429453243 (ebk)
Subjects: LCSH: Education—Effect of technological innovations on. | Educational technology—Study and teaching. | Internet in education.
Classification: LCC LB1028.3 .Z544 2019 | DDC 371.33—dc23
LC record available at https://lccn.loc.gov/2018043344

ISBN: 978-1-138-32050-5 (hbk)
ISBN: 978-1-138-32051-2 (pbk)
ISBN: 978-0-429-45324-3 (ebk)

Typeset in Bembo
by Apex CoVantage, LLC

MIX
Paper from
responsible sources
FSC® C013056
www.fsc.org

Printed and bound in Great Britain by
TJ International Ltd, Padstow, Cornwall

"For in the end it is only the mind
that brings every technology to life."

Johann Wolfgang von Goethe

Contents

Preface

Digitalization has dominated the discourse in nearly all fields of human thought and action more completely than practically any other topic in recent years. Whether in the context of trade and industry, politics and administration, health and medicine, science and innovation, or school and instruction, digitalization is regarded as a key task for the future.

As understandable as this standpoint may be in the individual societal domains and as important as digitalization may appear, it is not entirely free of controversy. The philosopher Martin Heidegger expressed his doubts on the issue as early as 1954 in his work, *The Question Concerning Technology*, although he could not have imagined all the things technology is capable of today. In his search for the nature of technology, he arrives at an important conclusion: Technology can take away our freedom. His concern that technology can lead to dependency is legitimate and calls attention to the importance in the age of digitalization of not restricting our focus to possibilities but always also keeping its limits and dangers in mind.

As in the case of technology, digitalization should always be seen as nothing more than a means to an end. As soon as we see it as an end in itself and begin to lose ourselves in it, we need to exercise caution. When children spend more time in front of the computer than they do with their friends, when youths cannot go more than five minutes without checking their account for new messages, and when parents spend more time playing with their smartphone than with their children, then we need to be concerned.

This book is intended as a contribution to the discussion on this issue. The goal is to elucidate the possibilities and limits of digitalization in the context of education, and above all to identify the domains in which digital learning can provide an additional benefit as well as those in which it is definitely better to avoid learning digitally. Against this backdrop, the title of the German edition of this book, *Learning 4.0: Pedagogy before Technology*, was not meant as a provocation. The intention was rather to call attention to false assumptions in the process of combining pedagogy with technology that lead to them being given equal status. The resulting danger is that we lose sight of the main object of pedagogy: the human being. The responsibility of educators is always to cultivate the human being. The human being is consequently both the starting point and the end point. This principle must also apply to digitalization in education. The digital cannot serve as a replacement for the pedagogical. Rather, the digital must be subordinated to the pedagogical.

Writing a book necessarily involves exchanging ideas with a lot of different people, and this book is no exception. I would thus like to express my general gratitude to everyone whose input shines through in one passage or another. However, I would like to give special thanks to Josef Schätz, responsible for all questions concerning schools as director of education in the regional government of Lower Bavaria. He brought up the topic of digitalization with me again and again in our many discussions about school and instruction and invited me to attend various lectures. My reflection on these discussions ultimately led to the comprehensive overview of learning 4.0 presented in the following.

The first German edition of *Learning 4.0* came out in the summer of 2017. Since digitalization was one of the main issues of the ongoing parliamentary election campaign in Germany, it immediately attracted great interest. It received several reviews, and I published further articles on the topic in journals and daily newspapers, held lectures, gave interviews, and participated in discussion groups at various levels. Moreover, my research assistants and I at the University of Augsburg collaborated with the Hasso Plattner Institute to hold a MOOC on "Learning 4.0" as part of a project called "School Cloud," funded by the German Federal Ministry of Education and Research. All these activities allowed me to gain a wealth of experience concerning my own positions on digitalization and to collect a lot of feedback on them. That alone would have been reason enough to present a second edition after the first one sold out in the spring of 2018, but there was also another good reason for bringing the book up to date: John Hattie went over the data for the Visible Learning project again in late 2017 and added a list of more than 250 new factors, which he extracted from more than 1400 meta-analyses. In view of the current global interest in digitalization, it comes as no surprise that a number of these new factors are relevant in this context. I have added these factors to the second edition you are reading now, which has thus been revised and brought up to date not just in terms of its argumentation but also from an empirical standpoint. What has not changed is the main message: pedagogy before technology.

Against this background I am delighted to present the English version under the title *Putting Learning Before Technology! The Possibilities and Limits of Digitalization*. I invite you to engage critically and constructively with the ideas expounded upon in this book. If any of these ideas raises questions about your own life or about your own thoughts and action in educational contexts, then I will have achieved my goal.

Marklkofen, June 2018
Klaus Zierer

1

Digitalization between euphoria and apocalypse

Task for reflection

Reflect on what you already know about digitalization: What domains can you name in which digitalization is sparking a revolution? What domains can you name in which digitalization is falling short of the expectations originally placed in it? And how much importance do you attach to digitalization in education?

Goals

This chapter attempts to characterize digitalization as a focal point of public discourse. It describes the standpoints of those who are highly optimistic about digitalization as well as those who see digitalization more as a threat than a blessing. When you finish reading this chapter, you should be able to answer the following questions:

- What is the meaning of the term "digital natives," and what is the distinguishing feature of this generation?
- Is it legitimate to speak of a revolution in view of the developments in hardware and software in the past 10 to 20 years?
- What threats does digitalization pose for processes of learning and development?
- What is the current state of our knowledge about the possible effects of digitalization on human health?
- How digitized is our lifeworld?
- What conclusions does this allow us to draw for digitalization in education?

Promoting digitalization in all societal domains is currently among the top political priorities around the world. In a 2016 interview with talk show host Anne Will, for example, German Chancellor Angela Merkel stated that she had chosen digitalization as one of the key issues of her next term. It makes no difference what sector one is talking about—trade and industry, politics and administration, health and medicine, science and innovation, or school and instruction. The argumentation is the same in every case: Digitalization is a challenge for the future, and everyone is afraid of missing the boat.

This is of course also true of educational policy. The task of getting schools connected to the internet and equipping them with the necessary modern technology is on the agenda of every political party. One would be hard pressed to find a ministry of education anywhere on earth that has not launched an initiative in this area. In the German-speaking world, for instance, such proposals go by names like "media offensive," "learning 2.0," and "digital revolution." An initiative proposed in 2016 by the German Federal Minister of Education and Research Johanna Wanka has a similar thrust: It involves investing five billion euros to help turn 40,000 schools into digital learning institutions in the next five years. Although the funding was not yet available at the time the proposal was launched, this stance on digitalization was and remains a part of the political agenda.

For many, digitalization therefore constitutes the key step in the process of taking education and training into a new millennium. And yet it is not even clear what is meant by "digitalization." In public discourse the use of the term is imprecise, serving as a collective name for a number of recent technological developments: Is learning with a computer already digital learning, or does it have to be done on a tablet? Does work with interactive whiteboards count? And what about pocket calculators?

It is this lack of precision that makes the term "digitalization" seem appropriate for this book. After all, the technological developments of the past decades— the radio, the overhead projector, the pocket calculator, the tape recorder, the television, the interactive whiteboard, the smartphone, or the tablet computer— all have one thing in common: Opinions on them in public discourse oscillate between euphoria and apocalypse.

The associated hype surrounding "digital learning" is being driven by influential mass media, which invoke threatening scenarios time and again: The 47th issue of *Die Zeit* from the year 2014 proclaimed that "the digital world ends at the school gate," *Spiegel Online* from 12 December of the same year bemoaned "teachers without a connection," and as early as late October 2010 *Focus Online* asserted that "teachers are neglecting new media." The message is clear: Only by giving digital learning top priority in the classroom is it possible to conduct modern and successful educational work.

This reporting on educational policy makes a good many teachers feel as if they have their backs to the wall. They are worried, sometimes even afraid, that they have missed something and that they are doing a lot of things wrong. It will be a great comfort for these teachers to hear the critics who are less enthusiastic about digitalization. Besides, a closer look at these positions reveals that, in reality, quite a few of the promises made in the euphoria surrounding digitalization do not live up to expectations. Against this backdrop, it is no wonder that the pendulum in the discussion then rapidly swings back in the direction of a digitalization apocalypse. So what threads can we find in this conflict? What are the main messages, and how is it possible to resolve the tension between these two extremes?

As a means of finding an answer to these questions, I would like to present several theses and antitheses on digitalization in education in the following. Although the selection is by no means exhaustive, it does serve to reveal the scope of the discussion and the vehemence with which it is being conducted. In conclusion, I will attempt to bring the two views together in the form of a synthesis.

Thesis: Today's children are digital natives

It is one of the most common arguments advanced in the conflict between opponents and advocates of digitalization: The children and youths of today are digital natives. This thesis has been formulated by Marc Prensky (2010) among others and is uncontroversial at the following level: Children and youths now grow up in a world in which digitalization is a permanent fixture. Every household is equipped not just with radios, televisions, and telephones but also with computers, smartphones, and tablets. The use of new media and the internet is perfectly natural for both parents and their children, yet while the former have had to acquaint themselves with these technologies in the course of their lives, the latter were confronted with them from the time they were born. The theory of digital natives goes even further: First, it argues that older generations are in danger of becoming digital immigrants. Teachers in particular are at risk, because they cannot keep abreast of the experiences of the digital natives and are therefore not in the position to design learning processes for them. Second, this leads to the conclusion that learning itself has changed for digital natives. These two implications are untenable from an educational science perspective, as will be explained below. In the following, I would therefore like to take a look at the lifeworld of the digital natives, which has indeed changed (cf., on the following, Bundesministerium für Familie, Senioren, Frauen und Jugend, 2017).

One of the most important characteristics of the digitalization of a lifeworld is the dichotomy between freedom and necessity. On the one hand, digitalization enables us to overcome space and time and communicate with people at all times and in all places. The boundaries between space and time seem to disappear. Yet on the other hand, digitalization forces us to give up this freedom again: Being reachable everywhere and connected with many people also means being available all the time and everywhere. This makes digital communication and networking into a characteristic feature of childhood and youth, if not the most characteristic feature of all, and it should come as no surprise that companies see this feature as a market to exploit. As a consequence, nearly 100 percent of 12- to 25-year-olds now have their own smartphone and use it nearly every day to get on the internet. Youths themselves state that they use the internet for a variety of purposes. However, the amount of time they spend searching for information is negligible compared to the amount they spend on the areas of "entertainment" and "games," and they spend the most time of all by a wide margin on communication. Bearing in mind that youths have nearly 300 social contacts of this kind, it is evident how much their lifeworld has changed on account of digitalization and how the task of discovering one's identity has changed as a result (cf. Montag, 2018)—I will only allude to possible dangers here, such as cybermobbing, misuse of data, and manipulation.

Thesis: Today's hardware and software are revolutionary

The state of technological development has advanced at lightning pace in recent decades. As an example from the domain of computer technology, take the Zuse Z3, a wonder computer in its time that took up an entire room and was so expensive hardly anyone could afford it, and compare it with an ordinary laptop computer that can be purchased today at a relatively low price and taken along everywhere one goes.

Figure 1.1 Zuse Z3
Source: © Udo Bojahr, fotolia.com

Figure 1.2 Laptop
Source: © Christos Georghiou, fotolia.com

Just as the speed of technological development has accelerated, the amount of time it takes for technological innovations to be adopted has shortened. Whereas the radio needed several decades to become accepted and used by most people, the television only needed a single decade, the internet no more than a few years, and new apps need just a few weeks or months to conquer the market. Each of these innovations has the potential to unleash new possibilities for communicating and interacting.

Hence, the rate of change is increasing—and at such a pace that innovation cycles no longer last a number of years but just a few months, making them a challenge for each individual rather than the task of an entire generation. With this in mind, it is only logical that many people hold hopes that digitalization will open a view to unforeseen horizons.

Antithesis: Digitalization is harmful

It is perhaps only natural that (technological) advances give rise to criticism as well as approval. This is hence also true in the context of digitalization. Such criticism is interesting for the purposes of this book because it calls into question the pedagogical value of new media from the outset and may also involve argumentation to the effect that increasing digitalization could even prevent learning.

This phenomenon has been observed by educational researchers like Maryanne Wolf (2007) even just in the context of reading texts on the internet, since the World Wide Web also invites shifts in attention and harbors many different sources of distraction. This has even led some researchers to assume that extensive internet use can lead to concentration difficulties and work to the detriment of deep and complex thinking (cf. Hattie & Yates, 2015; Stetina & Kryspin-Exner, 2009). Neil Postman (1985, p. 157), a pioneer of modern technology criticism, once wrote of similar studies that "to make the assumption that technology is always a friend of culture is, at this late hour, stupidity plain and simple."

Nicolas Carr (2010) hence asks the provocative question: "Is Google making us stupid?" Here is an example that should be familiar to many readers: You travel to an unfamiliar city and can't find your way to the hotel. So the first thing you do is whip out your smartphone and launch an app to show you the way. This is a sure-fire way reach your goal quickly, but it also means you'll miss out on challenges like practicing your orientation skills and asking strangers for directions.

Pam A. Mueller and Daniel M. Oppenheimer (2014) conducted an interesting study in this connection, published under the title "The Pen Is Mightier Than the Keyboard." They investigated whether the memory performance of students is better when they use paper and pencil to take notes or when they use a laptop. The results are clear: Students who take their notes on paper perform better on both simple reproduction tasks and complex transfer tasks than students who use a laptop. As an explanation, the authors suggest that the students who work with paper and pencil are better at cognitively penetrating and structuring what they have heard, leading them to write down far fewer words. To put it bluntly: In comparison to traditional media, new media can also prevent learning.

Manfred Spitzer even goes one step further, predicting that new media will lead to the onset of a "digital dementia." Figure 1.3 attempts to sketch out the resulting nightmare in biographical sequence (Spitzer, 2014, p. 298).

The remedies Spitzer proposes include limiting children's access to new media by only allowing them to access age-appropriate content and giving them time limits, largely banishing information technology from schools, fostering learning through non-digital means, and concentrating on the real world.

The problem with digitalization, one might conclude upon reading Neil Postman's book *Amusing Ourselves to Death* (1985), is not that people are laughing instead of thinking. The problem is rather that they no longer know what they are laughing about and have stopped thinking about why.

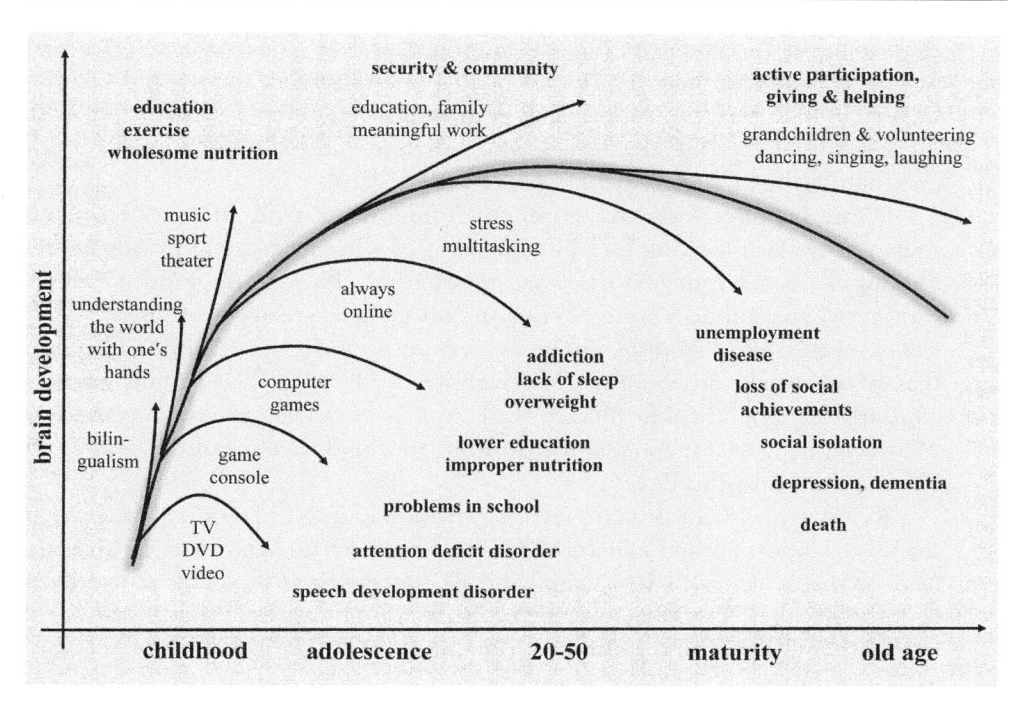

Figure 1.3 Risks of digitalization

Source: cf. Spitzer (2014)

Antithesis: Digitalization is unhealthy

A discussion of the pros and cons of digitalization would not be complete without mentioning an argument that oftentimes earns one the reputation of being a romantic, an old stick-in-the-mud, namely the fact that there are still a number of unsettled health issues surrounding digitalization, known under the term "electrosmog." To this day, we are still waiting for a study to provide conclusive evidence that constant exposure of our bodies to WLAN or mobile phone radiation cannot lead to (serious) health damage. Instead, there are a number of indications that the opposite is the case. A constant increase in attention disorders and psychosomatic illnesses in our society are clear signs that the conditions for life are changing, that they are becoming more hostile for humans (cf. Montag, 2018). Since new media doubtlessly represent one of the most far-reaching changes in the modern world, they should be viewed with a critical eye by the educational sciences.

Last but not least, the fact that a mobile phone and WLAN ban at schools was discussed by a Council of Europe committee in 2011 should also serve to curb some of the euphoria surrounding digitalization. The deliberations were preceded by several hearings in European Union member countries, including Germany. The basis for the hearings was a number of empirical studies providing indications that the electromagnetic radiation emitted by new media might present a health risk (cf. Moritz, 2011; Mutter, 2013).

If one searches for coverage of this topic in the daily press, one quickly finds what one is looking for. The question of whether radiation from mobile phones can cause cancer is discussed repeatedly: "New Study Finds Connection between Mobile Phone Radiation and Cancer" reads the title of a *Focus Online* article and "Mobile Phone Radiation Could Cause Tumor Growth" that of an article on the *Die Welt* website, both from 2016, while an article with the title "Mobile Phone Radiation Is Not Dangerous" appeared on *Merkur.de* in 2010. It is still not possible to conclusively confirm or refute either position to this day.

As a witty aside in this connection, I would like to call to mind an entry in the 2001 edition of the *Guinness World Records* on what is known in Japan as the "Pokémon shock": On 16 December 1997, more than 700 children had to be taken to hospital because an episode of the television cartoon show *Pokémon* had caused them to go into convulsions. A total of 208 children aged three years and up had to undergo inpatient treatment. According to experts, the convulsions were triggered by a scene in which lights flashed from the eyes of the character Pikachu (Birkelbach et al., 2001, p. 87).

Electromagnetic radiation is also one of the topics of Joachim Mutter's (2013) book *Lass dich nicht vergiften!* ("Don't Let Yourself Be Poisoned"), in which the environmental medicine specialist warns of the dangers of becoming overly reliant on technology.

Another aspect that should not be ignored in this connection is the issue of sustainability, which may be described in the words of Wolfgang Klafki (1996) as an "epoch-typical key problem." In other words, it is a problem that is faced in equal measure by all countries, a problem that connects the world in a chain of cause and effect, and a problem that currently demands to be taken seriously and be resolved. Generally speaking, it is possible to consider sustainability from an ecological, an economic, and a social perspective. Digitalization is not entirely uncontroversial from these perspectives. It opens up a new market and is in this sense economically interesting, but at the same time it destroys markets and leaves nothing in their place. It creates new avenues for communication and networking, but it also breeds anonymity on the one hand and allows invasions of privacy on the other. It can reduce the need for paper, but it also exploits limited resources, with more resources being consumed with each device owned by an individual. In the end, what this comparison shows is that the question as to whether digitalization promotes or hinders sustainability is essentially a question of how and why people use it.

How digitized is your lifeworld?

Before I come to a synthesis, I would like to provide the latest data on the state of digitalization of the lifeworld. *We Are Social* and *Hootsuite* publish an annual "Global Digital Report." A number of results will be presented below (cf. We Are Social & Hootsuite, 2018).

It has only been 25 years since Tim Berners-Lee made the "World Wide Web" available to the public. But in that time, the internet has already become an integral part of everyday life for most of the world's population. And it is not just the internet that's growing rapidly, either. We are living in a digital world.

First, a global view of digitalization:

In 2018 globally . . .

- over 4 billion people are internet users (up 7% compared to 2017; penetration 53%);
- over 3 billion people are active social media users (up 13% compared to 2017; penetration 42%);
- over 5 billion people are unique mobile users (up 4% compared to 2017; penetration 68%);
- nearly 3 billion people are active mobile social users (up 14% compared to 2017; penetration 39%);
- each user spends over six hours using the internet per day (all ages).

The statistics just presented are also interesting for America and Europe in detail. In 2018 in America . . .

- over 700 million people are internet users (up 3% compared to 2017; penetration 73%);
- over 600 million people are active social media users (up 8% compared to 2017; penetration 64%);
- over 1 billion people are unique mobile users (up 0.1% compared to 2017; penetration 106%);
- over 500 million people are active mobile social users (up 9% compared to 2017; penetration 57%);
- each user spends over six hours using the internet per day (all ages) in the USA.

In 2018 in Europe . . .

- over 600 million people are internet users (up 6% compared to 2017; penetration 80%);

- over 400 million people are active social media users (up 8% compared to 2017; penetration 53%);
- over 1 billion people are unique mobile users (up 0.5% compared to 2017; penetration 131%);
- nearly 400 million people are active mobile social users (up 8% compared to 2017; penetration 45%);
- each user spends over five hours using the internet per day (all ages) in the UK and over four hours in Germany.

The fact that these statistics can nevertheless be highly country-specific is shown, for example, by the internet penetration with regard to single countries (Table 1.1).

Similar statistics can be seen for social media use, in Table 1.2.

Impressive, but not surprising in view of the statistics presented, the constant increase in global monthly mobile data traffic totals over 10 billion GB (see Figure 1.4). A simple smartphone alone has an average of 2.9 GB of data traffic per month.

The conclusion of the authors of the Global Digital Report 2018 is therefore clear:

> With more than 4 billion people using the internet for an average of 6 hours each per day, digital has become an essential part of everyday life for most of us. We're using that connectivity in almost every aspect of our lives, whether it's chatting with friends, playing games, researching products, tracking our health, or even finding love.

Table 1.1 Internet penetration with regard to single countries

Rank	Country	Percentage	Users
1	Qatar	99%	2,640,360
2	United Arab Emirates	99%	9,376,171
3	Kuwait	98%	4,100,000
. . . UK 95%, Germany 91%, and USA 88% . . .			
211	Niger	4%	946,440
212	Eritrea	1%	71,000
213	North Korea	.06%	16,000

Table 1.2 Social media use with regard to single countries

Rank	Country	Percentage	Users
1	Qatar	99%	2,640,000
2	United Arab Emirates	99%	9,376,000
3	Kuwait	98%	4,100,000
. . . USA 71%, UK 66%, and Germany 46% . . .			
211	Eritrea	1%	53,000
212	Turkmenistan	1%	33,000
213	North Korea	.06%	16,000

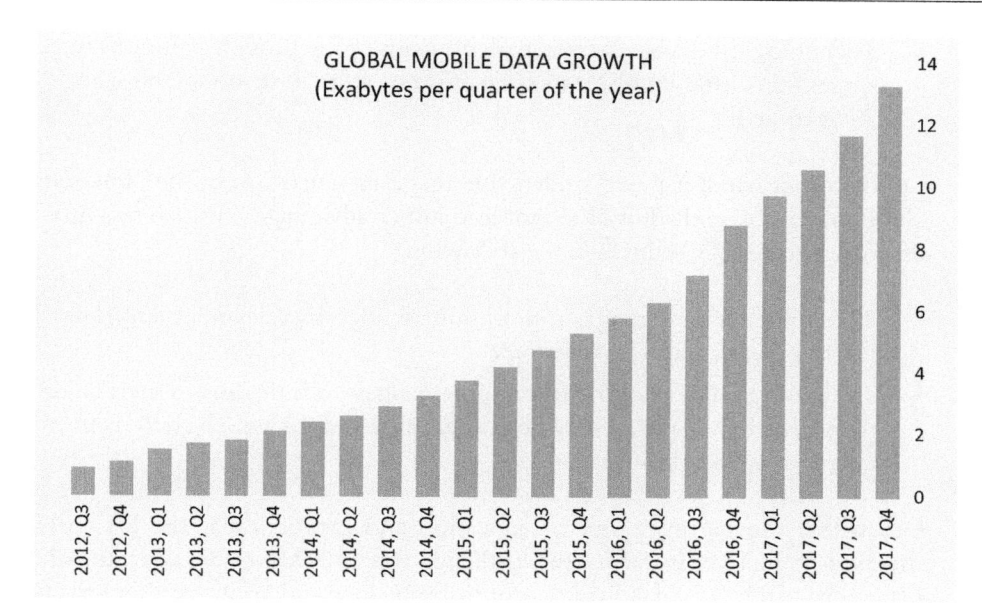

Figure 1.4 Global mobile data growth

Source: cf. We Are Social & Hootsuite (2018)

All these facts were incorporated into an interview Simon Sinek—leading management consultant and bestselling author—gave in 2016 (Sinek, 2016), in which he described the characteristics of the millennials. This video caused a lot of discussion within a very short period of time. One of his key statements was: The youth should reduce their exposure to technology, specifically mobile phones. Many of the elite in digitalization such as Steve Jobs and Evan Williams never allowed their children to use iPads or mobile phones knowing full well what the outcomes would be from constant usage. They were well aware of the correlation of addiction with technology and the dopamine that mobile phones release in our brains. That awareness was part of their climb to such global success. Simon Sinek's theses are certainly not uncontroversial. In essence, however, they show that digitalization per se is neither good nor bad. What matters most is what we human beings do with digitalization. In times of major transformations it is always helpful in my point of view to have apocalyptics as well as euphorics—because the truth lies between the extremes.

Synthesis: Digitalization is part of our lifeworld

What conclusions can be drawn from these various opposing positions? On the one hand, it is undeniable that digitalization is part of the lifeworlds of children and youths as well as adults today:

- Communication structures have changed. They follow other principles and hence open up new realms of possibility.

- Technological developments in all domains of life provide solutions to challenges that either involved massive effort or were insurmountable only 20 to 30 years ago.

On the other hand, it is also undeniable that a digitalization of the lifeworlds of children, youths, and adults does not lead just to advantages but also to a number of disadvantages. They include the following:

- The influence of digitalization on human cognitive development is not just positive but can also be negative.
- Technological developments can pose dangers to humans and their environment that may have already been identified but for which there is in many cases not yet a solution.

Given that the starting point of education and instruction is the lifeworld of the learners in all of its facets, the challenge this entails from an educational science perspective is to take into account both sides and confront them through pedagogical means, and therefore both use the advantages and remove the disadvantages. I will present the necessary steps for this in the next chapter. In the process, I will devote special attention to the concept of *Bildung* (i.e. formation or self-development), as this will provide the relevant background for reflecting on digitalization in the context of education and instruction. This is the key difference between an educational science approach and other perspectives on the issue, such as an economic approach.

Summary

WHAT IS THE MEANING OF THE TERM "DIGITAL NATIVES," AND WHAT IS THE DISTINGUISHING FEATURE OF THIS GENERATION?

"Digital natives" is a collective name for a generation that, in contrast to earlier generations, was born into a lifeworld in which digitalization is a permanent fixture. Hence, "digital natives" grow up in a world with computers, smartphones, tablets, and the internet. Unlike the digital natives, earlier generations have had to familiarize themselves with and learn to use all of these digital advances in the course of their lives.

IS IT LEGITIMATE TO SPEAK OF A REVOLUTION IN VIEW OF THE DEVELOPMENTS IN HARDWARE AND SOFTWARE IN THE PAST 10 TO 20 YEARS?

If one takes a look at the milestones of digitalization, the time it takes to develop technologies has been drastically reduced. Whereas it used to take several decades for a new technology to be developed and then adopted by society, today it is often just a matter of a few months.

As a consequence, the challenge of coping with the changes is not spread out over several generations but must be dealt with by each and every individual.

WHAT THREATS DOES DIGITALIZATION POSE FOR PROCESSES OF LEARNING AND DEVELOPMENT?

Despite unleashing numerous positive possibilities, digitalization also poses several threats. They often correspond in nature to the possibilities, which may be characterized together as forming a dichotomy between freedom and necessity. In addition, digitalization can have a negative impact on cognitive development, as indicated by studies on reading, attention spans, and concentration skills.

WHAT IS THE CURRENT STATE OF OUR KNOWLEDGE ABOUT THE POSSIBLE EFFECTS OF DIGITALIZATION ON HUMAN HEALTH?

The question of whether, and if so to what extent, digitalization has negative effects on human health is still a matter of controversy today. Ultimately, it is a matter of the validity of contrasting results from different studies.

HOW DIGITIZED IS OUR LIFEWORLD?

The world is becoming increasingly digital, whether in terms of internet users, active social media users, unique mobile users, or active mobile social users. The trend is rising in all these fields.

WHAT CONCLUSIONS DOES THIS ALLOW US TO DRAW FOR DIGITALIZATION IN EDUCATION?

Digitalization is a part of the lifeworlds of children, youths, and adults today. It should therefore be seen as a challenge for education and instruction that involves revealing possibilities as well as limits.

2

The challenge

Learning 4.0

Task for reflection

Reflect on what you see digitalization as capable of achieving in education: What significance does digitalization have for education? How does learning change as a result of digitalization? And what is meant by learning 4.0?

Goals

Taking the educational mission of schools as a starting point, I will attempt in this chapter to describe the task of a media education. In doing so, I will apply existing approaches to describe digital learning as learning 4.0. When you finish reading this chapter, you should be able to answer the following questions:

- What implications does digitalization have for the educational mission of schools?
- What domains does media education encompass?
- What is the distinctive quality of digital learning, and what is meant by learning 4.0?

If digitalization is indeed a part of the lifeworlds of children, youths, and adults in all societal domains, the task is then to react to it through pedagogical means. But that is not all: It is always also a pedagogical task to exert active and conscious influence on the learner's lifeworld. Pedagogical thinking and action is therefore always located along the coordinates of a field of conflict between reproduction and innovation (cf. Fend, 2006).

To maintain orientation in this field of conflict and avoid drifting off in one direction or the other, it is important to have a basic pedagogical idea and to explicate it. The concept of the German *Bildung* (i.e. formation or self-development) is well suited for this task, since it has a particularly long tradition and is therefore well defined. While this is not to say that it is entirely unproblematic, it should be noted that attempts to replace it with other terms—the most prominent example without doubt being the concept of competence—have made the problems larger rather than smaller.

What, then, is meant by the concept of *Bildung*? What conclusions does it enable us to draw for school and instruction? How does our concept of education change in the face of digitalization and what are the implications of these changes for digital learning? I will attempt in the following to answer these and other similar questions, the goal being to lay the groundwork for further considerations on teaching and learning and hence to tap into new realms of possibility for digitalization in education.

The educational mission of schools

The concept of *Bildung* is not just a technical term in the field of educational science but is also relevant for educational policy. There is an article in every state constitution in the Federal Republic of Germany describing the educational mission of schools. The remarkable thing about the inclusion of such an article is that it embeds school and instruction in a legal context, from where it is then defined on the basis of tasks and obligations.

In Bavaria, Germany, for example, the educational mission of schools is set out in Article 131 of the Bavarian State Constitution. Paragraph 1 states the following:

> The task of schools is not only to teach the students knowledge and abilities but also to develop their spirit and character.

The foundation for the understanding of *Bildung* behind this statement is the anthropological definition of the human being as a person. This idea is codified in Article 1 of the Basic Law for the Federal Republic of Germany with the statement that human dignity is inviolable. People therefore do not just have a capacity for education but also the responsibility to educate themselves. The implication for the context of school and instruction is the obligation to support every person in his or her educational process.

The emphasis on the areas of knowledge and ability on the one hand and spirit and character on the other calls attention to the fact that education should not be limited to individual areas of human existence but should rather apply to the entire personality in all of its facets. In addition to cognitive aspects, this also includes social, moral, aesthetic, motivational, and spiritual elements, as well as many others (cf. Gardner, 2013). Limiting education to just a few of these areas and possibly using the person in question as human capital for external purposes is consequently out of the question. Human beings have an intrinsic value that should not be called into question, and their education should therefore not be exploited.

These reflections provide a basis for defining the goal of education: As a human capacity and obligation, education has no goal outside of itself. *Bildung* is therefore about the person, about shaping a human being and his or her personality. This process is never completed, because we humans are constantly faced with the challenge of being who we are.

This goal is also binding with regard to digitalization, which should consequently always serve as a means to an end: The whole purpose of digitalization should be to support people in the process of their education. Whenever it becomes an end in itself, reduces people to human capital, uses people to achieve an external goal, or violates human dignity, it should be rejected on pedagogical grounds.

In order for digitalization to achieve this aim, it is necessary to see to it that people receive a comprehensive media education that addresses the possibilities as well as the limits of digitalization and that qualifies them to assess for themselves where these possibilities and limits lie.

Media education as the goal

I have already pointed out that the concept of *Bildung* is not undisputed and that attempts have been made to replace it with other terms. These discussions do not always serve to make the issue clearer and more understandable; what they often lead to is rather a mishmash of terms that Wolfgang Brezinka (1990) sees as symptomatic of educational science. This is also true within the context of digitalization, where the terms vying for attention include digital education, digital learning, media competence, and media education, to name just a few.

Without attempting to untangle the intricacies associated with this debate, I will focus in the next paragraphs on the term "media education," for the following reasons.

First of all, the term takes up the tradition and thus the whole breadth of the debate surrounding the concept of *Bildung*. The focus should be on the human being, also or especially in the case of digitalization.

Second, unlike competence the term is not characterized by an empirical dominance. While empirical knowledge is important, it is also dangerous if not adequately grounded in theory.

Third, the term makes it clear that although digitalization is a modern phenomenon, it is rooted in a tradition which has always been discussed under the category of media; it has therefore already received broad critical attention; and the term also highlights the role of digitalization as a medium and therefore as a means to an end.

To characterize media education in more detail, I would like to begin by applying the concept of *Bildung* to a distinction made by Dieter Baacke (1997).

Baacke distinguishes between four fields that may be seen as representing subdomains of media education (Figure 2.1).

The first field, media knowledge, includes everything one needs to know to work with media. The second field, media use, refers to the ability to work with media. The third field, media production, encompasses all of the knowledge and abilities that are important for not just being a user of media but also modifying it to serve one's own aims and purposes. The fourth and last field, media criticism, involves the ability to take a self-regulatory and self-critical perspective toward media, with regard to both one's own use of it and that of society as a whole.

The following ideas on the topic "internet" are intended to clarify these thoughts:

Media criticism:

• Is everything true that is on the internet?

• What happens to my data?

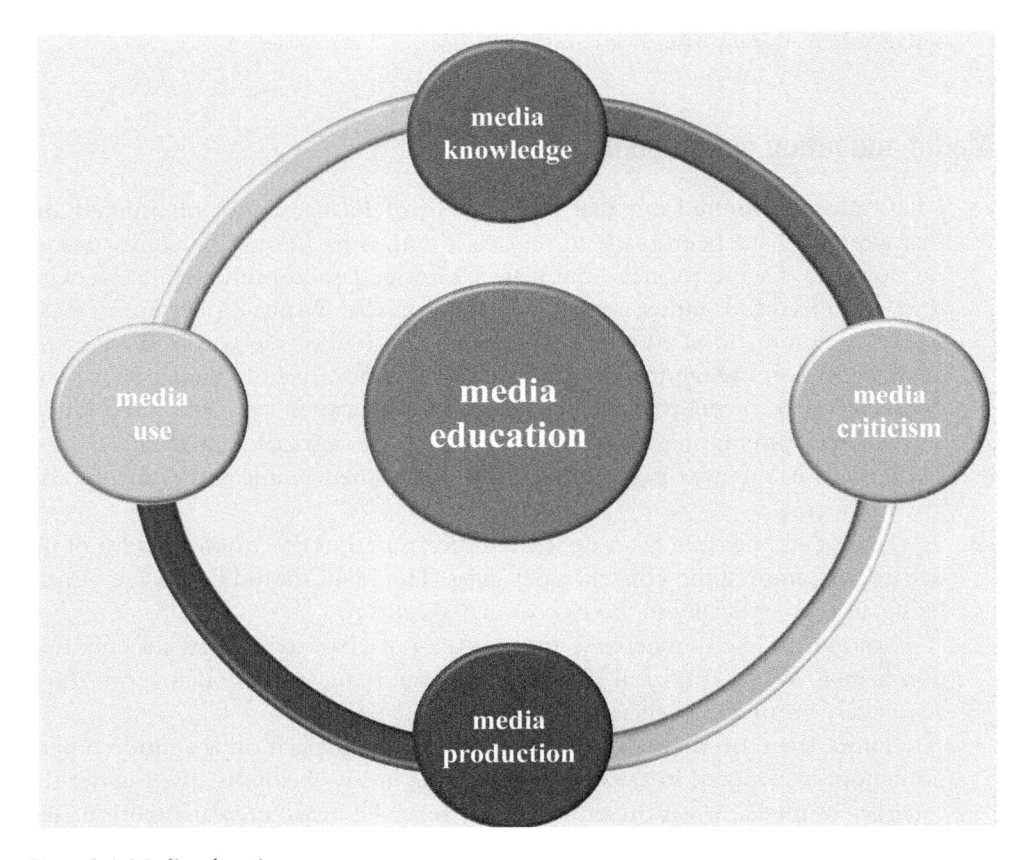

Figure 2.1 Media education
Source: cf. Baacke (1997)

- What do I do and who do I contact if I find strange things on the internet or get caught in cost traps?
- Keep a critical distance: recognize commercial interests.
- Being able to take responsibility and reflect on my own actions: apologizing for insults or standing up for cyberbullying.

Media knowledge:

- How do I find the information I'm looking for?
- What is the internet? What are the technical connections?
- Knowing and using the internet: using a browser.
- Being able to orientate and move on the internet: understand what a hypertext structure is and how to navigate it.

Media use:

- How do I communicate with others and how do I behave fairly in interactive offers?
- What do I do if I get bullied?
- Which data of mine may I disclose, what do I do if I get to problematic sites?
- Children must learn what it means to behave safely on the internet.
- Participate in digital forms of communication: chat or write a comment.

Media production:

- How and where can I be creative on the internet?
- How do I edit a photo and how and where can and may I put it online?
- What do other children say about my own stories?
- What will my homepage look like?
- Be creative on the web yourself: write a contribution and put it online.

What this selection of subdomains of media education clearly shows is, first, that media is always regarded as a means to an end; second, that the subdomains can influence each other; and third, that it is not just the areas of knowledge and ability that are important for media education but also those of will and judgment.

In light of the argumentation up to this point, consider the following definition: Media education is a domain of the educational mission of schools that concentrates essentially on the subdomains of media knowledge, media use, media production, and media criticism. Since these subdomains interact, they cannot be separated from one another entirely in practice, although each of them is distinguishable in theory. What may be defined as the main goal of media education is that it should qualify people to identify the possibilities offered by media and make meaningful use of them, while at the same time putting them in the position to perceive and avoid potential threats posed by media. This requires competencies, but it also requires mind frames.

Digital learning

The ideas set forth above indicate that a media education needs to cover a broad spectrum of topics. It is not possible in the context of this book to treat all of these topics in detail, as many of them would cause us to stray too far from the issue at hand. Take the subdomain of media knowledge, for example. The skills involved in operating computers, tablets, and other devices, the possibilities of programming apps, and the technical background of networking via the cloud are all issues that play no part in the following.

Moreover, some of the topics do not need to be covered in depth because they have already been discussed extensively elsewhere. Examples include the discussion of the importance of media pedagogy in the context of general pedagogy or the special role media didactics can play in connection with general didactics.

Digital learning, on the other hand, is an issue the discussion urgently needs to be steered toward. Teachers are confronted each and every day with the challenge of integrating into their lesson the myriad possibilities presented by the digitalization of our lifeworlds. This challenge is further intensified by a host of educational policy initiatives, such as those mentioned at the beginning of this book. What, then, is digital learning? What sets it apart from learning in other fields, from non–digital learning? Is digital learning a "learning 4.0," and what, exactly, does this mean? Or is this "learning 4.0" just a meaningless buzzword?

It seems sensible to begin by approaching the concept of learning. It involves three core aspects (cf., on the following, Weber, 1999):

- Learning effects changes in the behavioral and experiential possibilities available to the learner.
- These changes in behavioral and experiential possibilities in the course of learning come about as a result of experience (information processing) rather than as a result of primarily organic processes (e.g., maturation).
- Learning concerns not just the domains of knowledge, ability, capacities, and skills but also those of judgment, mind frames, attitudes, and much more.

Learning thus refers to a relatively permanent change in individual areas of personality on the basis of experiences. When we speak of a digital learning, we emphasize that this learning is based on experiences made possible with the help of digitalization. Two examples of digital learning in this sense are learning with the help of tablets or through the exchange of information on the internet.

These examples already demonstrate the diversity of digital learning, but they say nothing about what sets it apart from other forms of learning. Figure 2.2, which was introduced to illustrate the differences between versions 1.0 through 4.0 of the World Wide Web, offers a suitable means of demonstrating the distinctive quality of digital learning.

The main idea is that the degree of social connectivity on the one hand and that of information connectivity on the other increase with each new version. While Web 1.0 is characterized by a low degree of social and cognitive connectivity, the special thing about Web 4.0 is that it features a high degree of both social and cognitive connectivity. By way of explanation, consider the following example: A company that makes information available to the public on its website generates a low degree of information flow in a single direction and also establishes a one-sided connectivity. In comparison, a company that

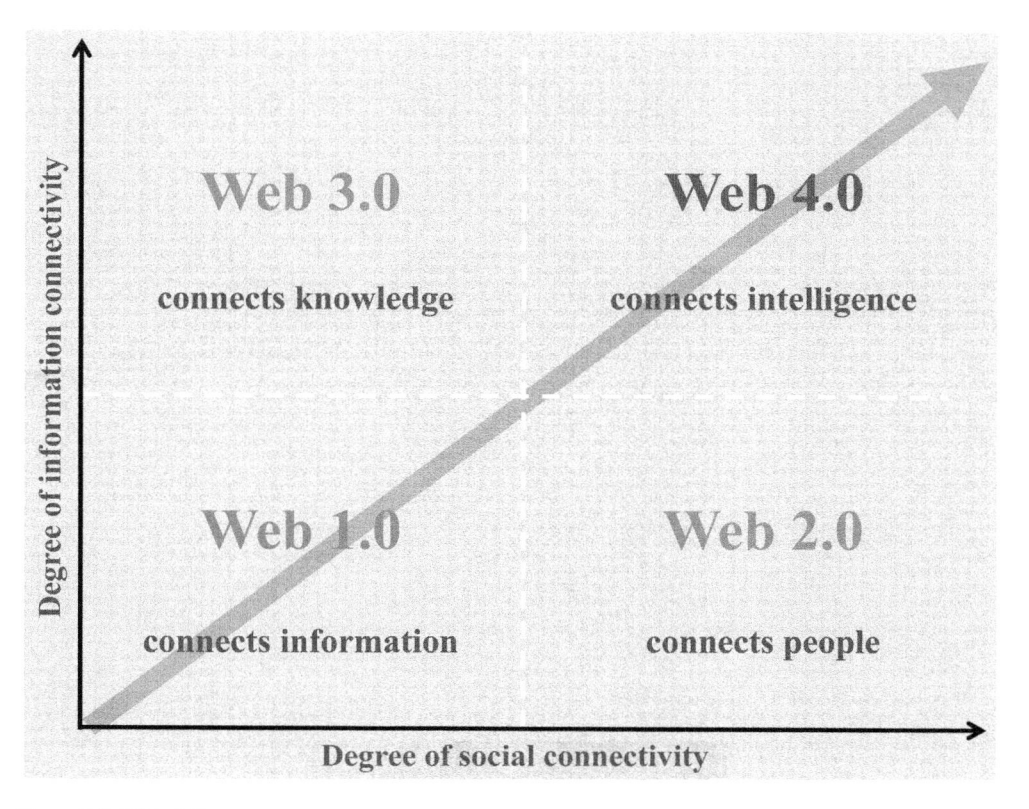

Figure 2.2 Web 4.0

Source: cf. Spivack (2017) and Wheeler (2017)

offers a contact form on its website already provides more social connectivity in both directions, and it can extend this connectivity further by integrating features like a communication platform for registered customers. If this platform also offers the possibility for all registered customers to exchange ideas and work on improving products together, then it also enables a higher degree of cognitive connectivity.

Web 4.0 is accordingly, in contrast to Web 1.0, an open system marked by social and cognitive connectivity and thus by exchange and cooperation.

This distinction may also be applied to learning. Learning 1.0 may therefore be described as a type of learning marked by a low degree of social and cognitive connectivity, whereas learning 4.0 is characterized by a strongly developed social and cognitive connectivity. Digital learning has the objective of being a learning 4.0, because it views this connectivity as benefiting learning. It should be noted, however, that digital learning is not always a learning 4.0 but can also be a learning 1.0. Moreover, it should be pointed out that digital learning is not the only path to achieving learning 4 0, but that many traditional forms of learning can also penetrate into this domain.

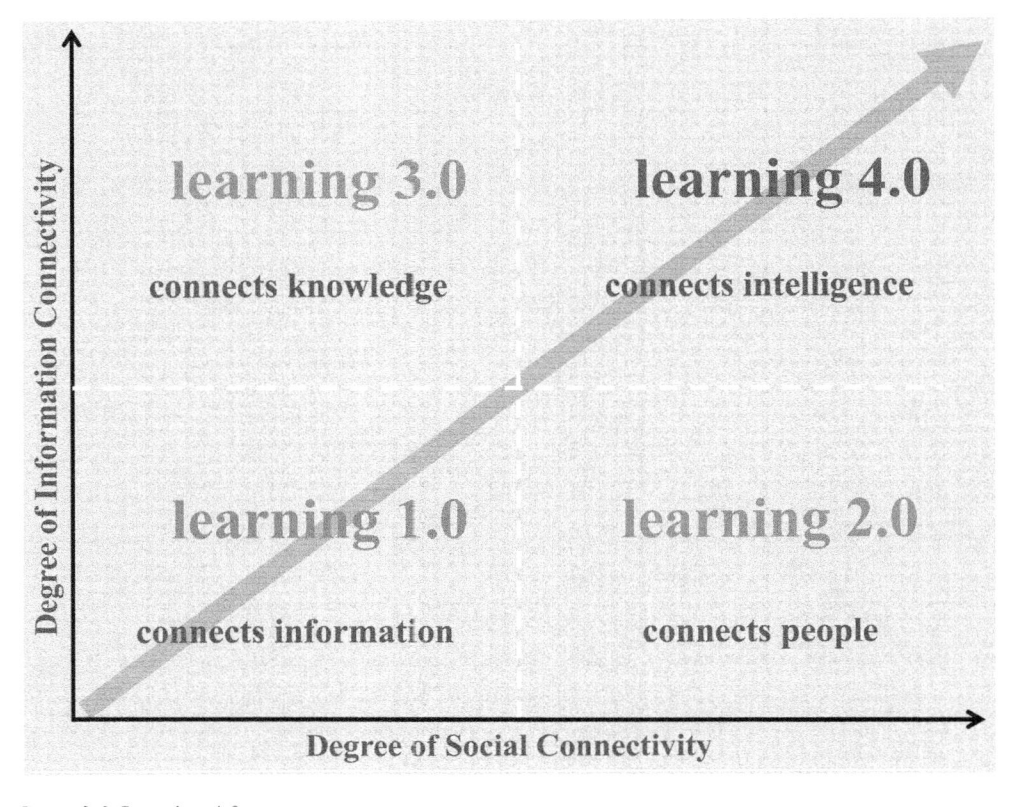

Figure 2.3 Learning 4.0

As a means of elucidating this idea further, consider the following two examples: When a learner reviews tasks he or she is already capable of completing, virtually no social or cognitive connectivity takes place—regardless of whether the learner reviews the task on a piece of paper or on a tablet computer. By contrast, a learner who works on a task together with several other persons and takes up their ideas and thoughts shows a high degree of cognitive and social connectivity. Traditionally, this has often occurred in out-of-school learning settings and projects, and in the age of digitalization it may be found in digital communication and cooperation forums.

Summary

WHAT IMPLICATIONS DOES DIGITALIZATION HAVE FOR THE EDUCATIONAL MISSION OF SCHOOLS?

The educational mission of schools involves not just reacting to social conditions but also addressing them proactively, and this means serving not just the function of reproduction but also that of innovation. Digitalization is doubtlessly part of the lifeworlds of children, youths, and adults today. Schools are therefore called upon to acknowledge this fact and develop a pedagogical approach for addressing it as part of their educational mission.

WHAT DOMAINS DOES MEDIA EDUCATION ENCOMPASS?

Media education may be seen as a central term for the challenge of examining the possibilities and limits of digitalization in education from a pedagogical perspective. It includes the subdomains of media knowledge, media use, media production, and media criticism.

WHAT IS THE DISTINCTIVE QUALITY OF DIGITAL LEARNING, AND WHAT IS MEANT BY LEARNING 4.0?

Digital learning involves learning processes that are initiated primarily on the basis of experiences with new media. If digital learning leads to high social and cognitive connectivity, it may be referred to as learning 4.0. This is where the greatest potential for digitalization in education lies, although it should be pointed out that non-digital learning can also be a form of learning 4.0.

3

What do we know about the influence of new media on the academic performance of children and youths?

Task for reflection

Reflect on what influence digitalization in instruction has on learning performance. Perhaps you have already integrated a computer, a tablet, an interactive whiteboard, or a smartphone into one of your lessons. Perhaps you have shown a learning video or filmed one yourself with your students. How effective were these measures for the learning outcome?

Goals

This chapter will present findings from empirical research that attempt to gauge the influence of digital learning. It will focus in particular on the Visible Learning meta-study by John Hattie, currently the most extensive effort to interpret the immense pool of educational studies. When you finish reading this chapter, you should be able to answer the following questions:

- What procedure is applied in Visible Learning?
- What are the general results regarding digital learning?
- What effect do the factors "web-based learning," "visual/audio-visual methods," "programmed instruction," "use of calculators," "computer-assisted instruction," "one-on-one laptops," "mobile phones," "use of PowerPoint," "interactive video methods," "intelligent tutoring system," and "technology with learning-needs students" have on learning outcomes?

- What is the main message of previous research on digitalization in school and instruction?
- Why is learning still learning?

Although digitalization may be seen as a recent phenomenon, it is not entirely new. On the contrary, it is part of a greater wave of technologization reaching far back into the 20th century and thus has a number of forerunners. It is an open issue as to whether the radio, the television, or the telephone may be seen as a part of this wave or not. It is beyond question that these technologies bear mentioning in this context, however, because digitalization is what catapulted the radio, the television, and the telephone into the digital age.

If we take a look at this issue in the context of educational science, we find such an abundance of studies on the possibilities and limits of digitalization in education that it is nearly impossible to sift through them all. It is therefore necessary to turn to attempts at deriving a synthesis. The most ambitious of these attempts is the Visible Learning project by John Hattie, which assembles and interprets a vast number of meta-analyses on the current state of educational research. In the following, I will present the most important points of Visible Learning and illustrate the core messages with regard to digital learning. In doing so, I will take a closer look at several factors and related primary studies. They are "web-based learning," "visual/audio-visual methods," "programmed instruction," "use of calculators," "computer-assisted instruction," "one-on-one laptops," "mobile phones," "use of PowerPoint," "interactive video methods," "intelligent tutoring system," and "technology with learning-needs students." Finally, I will attempt to derive a general conclusion from the multitude of research findings.

There is of course no guarantee that this will enable us to foresee the impact of all possible technological innovations—taking a look back is surely one of the great weaknesses of investigating educational reality through empirical means. Nevertheless, results obtained in this manner can make the structures of success and failure visible, and these structures can in turn provide grounds for evaluating the value of technological innovations on the one hand and for selecting appropriate ones for instructional practice on the other.

Taking Visible Learning as a basis

Attempt for a moment to determine how many studies have been conducted on the topics "homework," "teacher–student relationships," or "feedback." You will quickly realize that we are by no means suffering from a lack of studies and findings at the moment. On the contrary, we already possess a practically unmanageable pool of studies on these topics, and the findings could hardly be more disparate. In the case of homework, for instance, you will find studies proving that homework assignments have only a small effect on student learning performance, but you will also find studies proving that homework assignments have a large effect on student learning performance. So which of these studies are right?

In a similar fashion, you might try out the following little experiment: Go to a school and ask the members of the teaching staff individually what they think is the best way to teach. You will receive more than one answer to your question. It is safe to say that you will receive five or six different answers, or perhaps even ten or more.

These examples show that there is a large stockpile of knowledge available in education but that it is unfortunately not always entirely clear what knowledge is important and what knowledge is not important. This leads to myth-making, and the discussion on school and instruction is full of such myth-making: "Open instruction is better than closed instruction," "the teaching is better in small classes," and "comprehensive schools are better than a multipartite school system," to name just three examples.

An evidence-based approach is a helpful way to counteract this myth-making, because it does not ask merely whether there is a significant correlation between two aspects but also how large and meaningful a significant effect is. The Visible Learning meta-study typifies this approach more than any other study. It is the world's largest collection of empirical educational data, compiled by John Hattie in the course of more than 15 years of research and interpretation (cf. Hattie, 2013 and 2014; Hattie & Zierer, 2017; see also Zierer, 2014).

The findings of the first edition of *Visible Learning* from 2009 were based on more than 800 meta-analyses comprising around 80,000 studies in which an estimated 250 million learners took part. The result was a ranking of 138 factors. It is still important today to point out these numbers: If one compares them with the numbers from PISA, a study that has dictated the international discourse of educational policy in the past years and includes only around nine million learners, it becomes clear how ambitious the scope of Visible Learning is.

John Hattie has continued to update and expand his dataset in the intervening years. By the time *Visible Learning for Teachers* was published in 2010, it already included 150 factors extracted from more than 900 meta-analyses. Finally, in 2017 he presented a new edition of his dataset, now encompassing more than 1400 meta-analyses and a list of 250 factors assigned to the domains "student," "home," "school," "classroom," "teacher," "curricula," "teaching/ instruction strategies," "focus on implementation method," and "student learning strategies." The increase in factors concerned with digital learning is in itself remarkable, rising from six in 2009 to 24 today.

Visible Learning seeks to get to the crux of this multitude of findings from educational research and identify the main messages by synthesizing meta-analyses. This involves first generating more than 250 factors from the underlying meta-analyses, such as "class size," "teacher–student relationships," "direct instruction," and "feedback," and then determining their effect size, which is generally stated as d and refers to a statistical unit of measurement. A positive effect size means that the factor leads to an increase in learner performance, and a negative effect size means that the factor leads to a reduction in learner performance. If one takes this naive yet perfectly correct assumption for interpreting effect sizes and combines it with the frequency with which these effect sizes were found in the numerous meta-analyses, one obtains the representation shown in Figure 3.1 (cf. Zierer, 2014, and Hattie & Zierer, 2017).

An initial conclusion suggested immediately by Figure 3.1 is important: Nearly everything that happens at school and in the classroom leads to an increase in academic performance. To put it in another way, in 95 percent of cases students are smarter when they leave school than they were when they started school. One might think that this would reassure us teachers, but this is not the case. The only thing this result illustrates is that people are learning all the time. In other words, anything goes. It does not matter whether we introduce a new curriculum or not, because either way we will end up with a positive effect size. And it does not matter whether we have a comprehensive, bipartite, tripartite, quadripartite, or a quinquepartite system of secondary education, because we will always end up with a positive effect size. To put it bluntly: You cannot prevent learning.

The interpretation of factors in Visible Learning therefore involves not just asking whether the effect size is positive or negative. Rather, the meta-study argues that the bar should be set higher, namely at 0.4. Why 0.4? This value represents the average of all effect sizes measured in Visible Learning and as such marks the domain of "desired effects." It is generally equated with the average

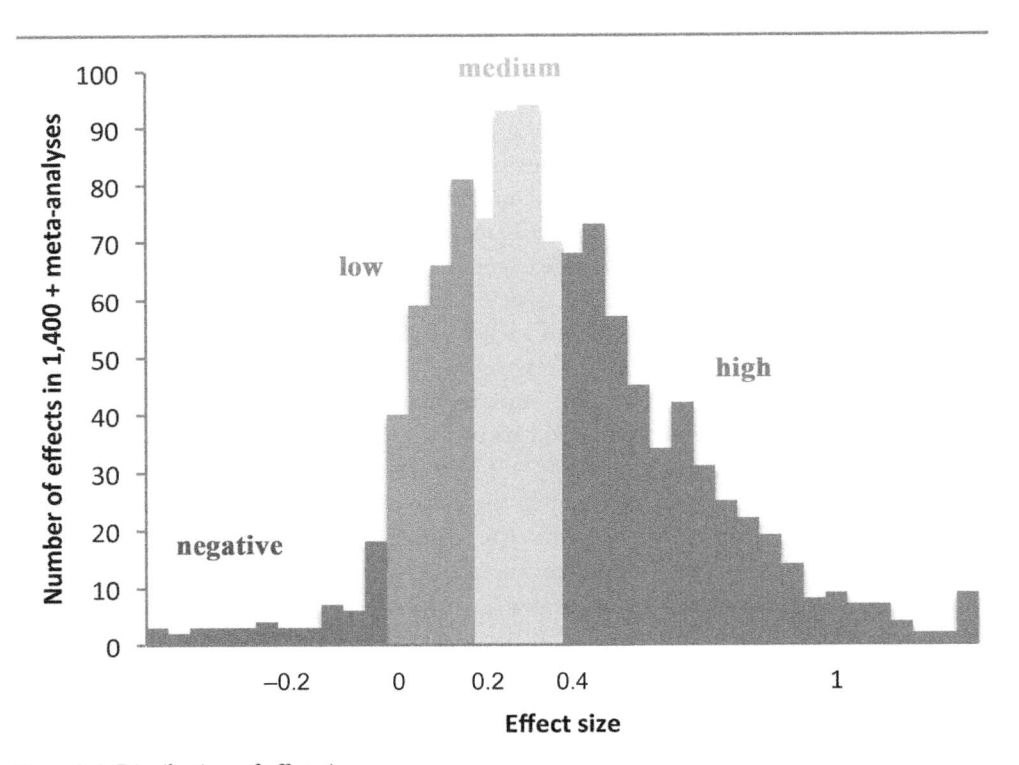

Figure 3.1 Distribution of effect size

yearly increase in student learning performance. What the study demands is therefore simple, but it is in my opinion convincing: Be better than average! Setting the bar at this level makes sense when one considers that humans learn automatically as they grow older. These learning effects are described as "developmental effects" and have effect sizes of between 0 and 0.2. It therefore follows that values between 0.2 and 0.4 may be described as ordinary "school effects" achievable at an average school, with an average teacher, in an average class, and with average parents. Negative effects—which seem particularly problematic but appear only seldom in reality—are referred to as "reverse effects." They occur only occasionally, but this does not make them any less interesting. This system for classifying effect sizes may be illustrated with the help of the barometer of influence shown in Figure 3.2, here for the factor "class size".

These considerations form the empirical foundation for the further argumentation presented in this book. Whenever possible, I will draw on them to back up my argumentation, the aim of which will thus be to produce evidence in the shape of a large effect size as a criterion for selecting important factors. In the process, however, it will also be necessary to keep in mind that factors with small effect sizes can be interesting too. One often needs to understand why a

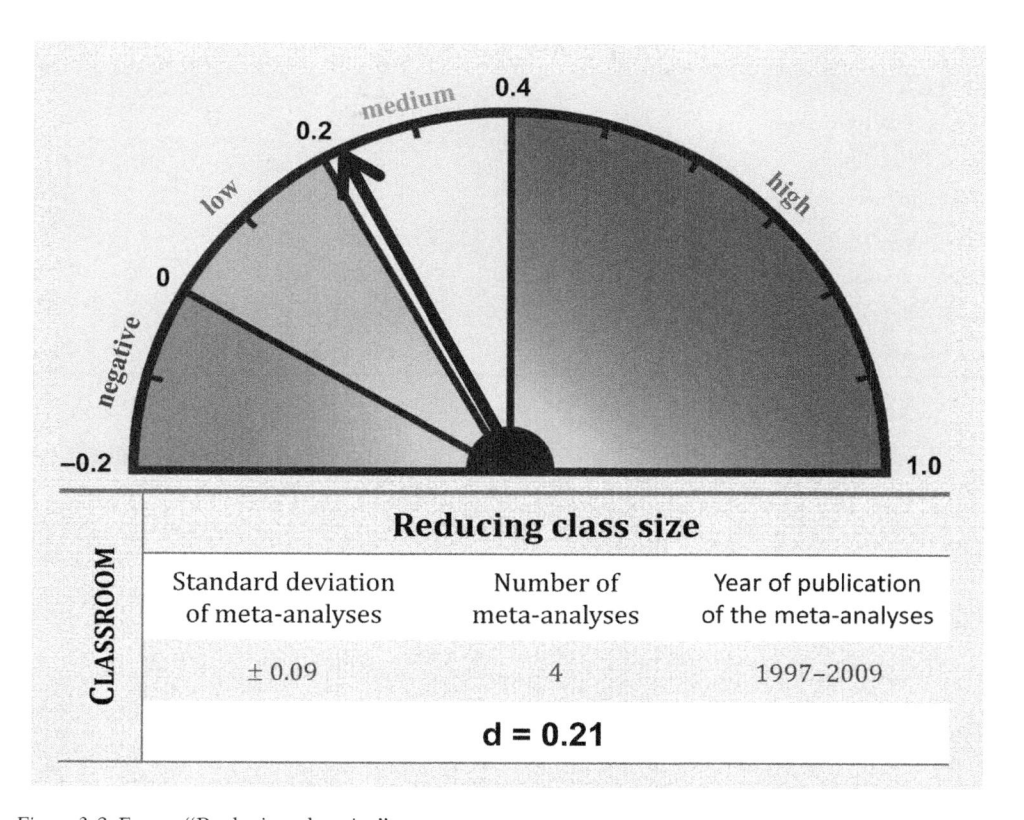

Figure 3.2 Factor "Reducing class size"

Table 3.1 Self-reflection of digitalization factors

	negative	*low*	*medium*	*high*
Clicker	○	○	○	○
Computer-assisted instruction	○	○	○	○
Technology in distance education	○	○	○	○
Technology in mathematics	○	○	○	○
Technology in other subjects	○	○	○	○
Technology in reading/literacy	○	○	○	○
Technology in science	○	○	○	○
Technology in small groups	○	○	○	○
Technology in writing	○	○	○	○
Technology with college students	○	○	○	○
Technology with elementary students	○	○	○	○
Technology with high school students	○	○	○	○
Technology with learning-needs students	○	○	○	○
Interactive video methods	○	○	○	○
Intelligent tutoring system	○	○	○	○
Mobile phones	○	○	○	○
Use of calculators	○	○	○	○
Programmed Instruction	○	○	○	○
Use of PowerPoint	○	○	○	○
Visual/audio-visual methods	○	○	○	○
Web-based learning	○	○	○	○
Gaming/simulation	○	○	○	○
Online, digital tools	○	○	○	○
One-on-one laptops	○	○	○	○

factor that is important for other reasons has so little influence in reality if one wishes to enhance its effect in the next step. Consequently, what I am after in essence is understanding, namely an understanding of empirical data in order to make it useful for classroom practice.

Before you read the next section, please reflect again on how effective you judge the factors in Table 3.1 to be.

General results on digital learning

Gaining a sense of orientation is becoming ever more difficult in view of this long list of factors on digital learning, including an increase from 138 to 150 and finally to more than 250 factors today and almost four times the amount of factors concerning digitalization. One might be inclined to conclude that Visible Learning is increasingly falling victim to the problem it was originally designed to solve, namely bringing some clarity into the broad fund of empirical educational research and making it more manageable. It will hence be necessary to engage in further structuring and interpretation if we wish to derive general results. Only on the basis of these general results will it make sense to take a look at individual factors.

In the following, I would like to venture an attempt of this kind for the 24 factors from the area of digitalization. My inquiry will be guided by three questions that play a role in the public discourse: What influence do 1) age, 2) subject, and 3) technology have on digital learning?

Table 3.1A

Factor	Effect size
Technology with elementary students	0.44
Technology with high school students	0.30
Technology with college students	0.42

1   The effect sizes of the factors concerning digitalization in the primary, secondary, and tertiary stages of education demonstrate that there is neither a continuous increase nor a continuous decrease of influence over various age groups. This would be the condition for concluding that there is a connection between age and the influence of digitalization on learning. An example of such an age-related increase is the factor "cooperative learning," which produces greater effects as the age of the learners increases (cf. Zierer, 2014, and Hattie & Zierer, 2017).

Table 3.1B

Factor	Effect size
Technology in mathematics	0.33
Technology in science	0.23
Technology in other subjects	0.55
Technology in reading/literacy	0.29
Technology in writing	0.42

2   This overview reveals that digitalization achieves only small effect sizes in the natural sciences and mathematics—a result that is in my mind surprising, as these two subjects may be described as lending themselves to digitalization. Just as surprising are the results for reading and writing: Whereas digitalization evidently has a good deal of potential for helping learners with their writing, it has only little impact on their reading skills.

Table 3.1C

Factor	Effect size
Clicker	0,22
Computer-assisted instruction	0.47
Mobile phones	0.37
Use of calculators	0.27
Use of PowerPoint	0.26
Visual/audio-visual methods	0.22
Web-based learning	0.18
Online, digital tools	0.29
One-on-one laptops	0.16

3   One of the most persistent arguments in the discussion on the possibilities and limitations of digitalization in education is that it is only a matter of time until technology revolutionizes learning. Even just a glance at Table 3.1C reveals that this is not necessarily the case. After all, most of the factors involving the more recent advances of the digital age, such as "one-on-one laptops," "online digital tools," "web-based learning," and "clickers," have only a small effect on learning. The only factor on this list that achieves an effect above the bar of 0.4 is "computer-assisted instruction."

What general results can we glean from the influence of age, subject, and technology on the effectiveness of digital learning? As it is not possible to derive any correlations from the data for any of these three aspects, we may assume that they are not decisive for the success of digitalization. Rather, these results already point in a clear direction: More important than age or subject or technology is the issue of how the teacher succeeds in integrating digital learning into the lesson. A detailed look at a selection of factors and related primary studies can serve to substantiate this essential point.

The factor "Web-based learning"

The factor "web-based learning" includes methods that use the internet as a medium. Although this domain may still seem too new to offer much in the way of pedagogical interventions, there are already a number of studies on web-based learning—and more are being conducted all the time. The effect size of 0.18 they achieve in the three meta-analyses seems small at first glance, but a closer look reveals that the effectiveness of such methods varies widely, indicating that there are differences in the way they are implemented. One key point that has been identified as a cause of the heterogeneous results is that programmers often have no pedagogical training, and this increases the potential for mistakes at the level of software. Multiprofessional teams can help to alleviate this problem.

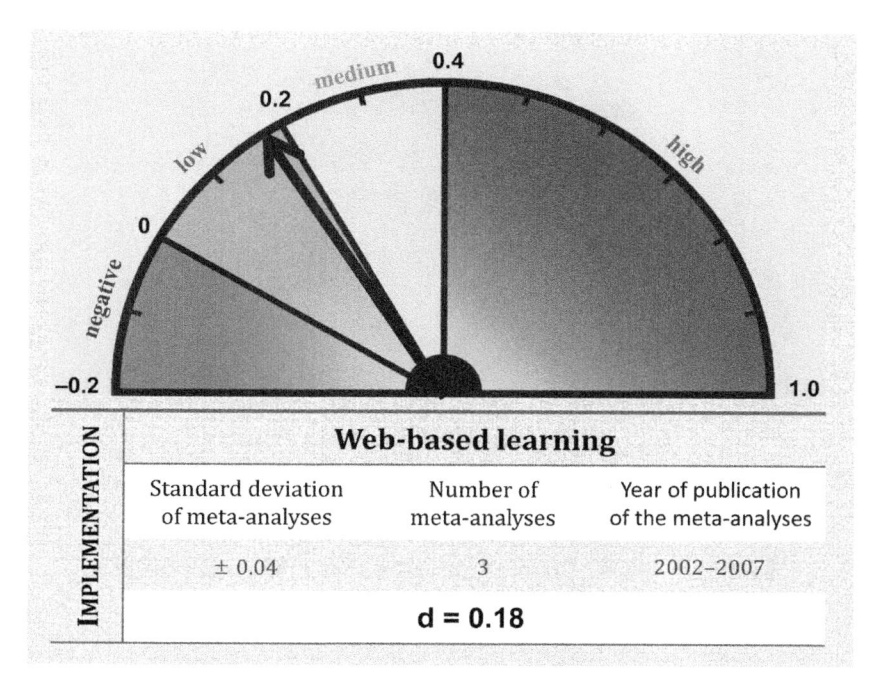

IMPLEMENTATION	**Web-based learning**		
	Standard deviation of meta-analyses	Number of meta-analyses	Year of publication of the meta-analyses
	± 0.04	3	2002–2007
	d = 0.18		

Figure 3.3 Factor "Web-based learning"

The factor "Visual/audio-visual methods"

The factor "visual/audio-visual methods" unites meta-analyses dealing with technological innovations of the past 30 to 40 years. It focuses among other things on the use of modern visual and audio-visual media to support learning. This includes the tape recorder, radio, television, film, and multimedia applications, as well as more recent innovations like beamers and interactive whiteboards. These methods achieve an overall effect size of 0.22. One of the main messages of the primary studies is that new media often serve merely as a replacement for traditional media, for instance the interactive whiteboard or the beamer as a replacement for the blackboard. Hence, whatever potential these technologies might have either has yet to be discovered or is at least not being exploited to its full potential.

The factor "Programmed instruction"

The factor "programmed instruction" includes concepts that involve organizing the learning material into a sequence and having the learners work it through step by step depending on their achievement level. Initially developed for paper and pencil, these methods have been developed further to incorporate the possibilities offered by hardware and software in the classroom. They achieve an average effect size of 0.23 and therefore fall short of expectations. The important

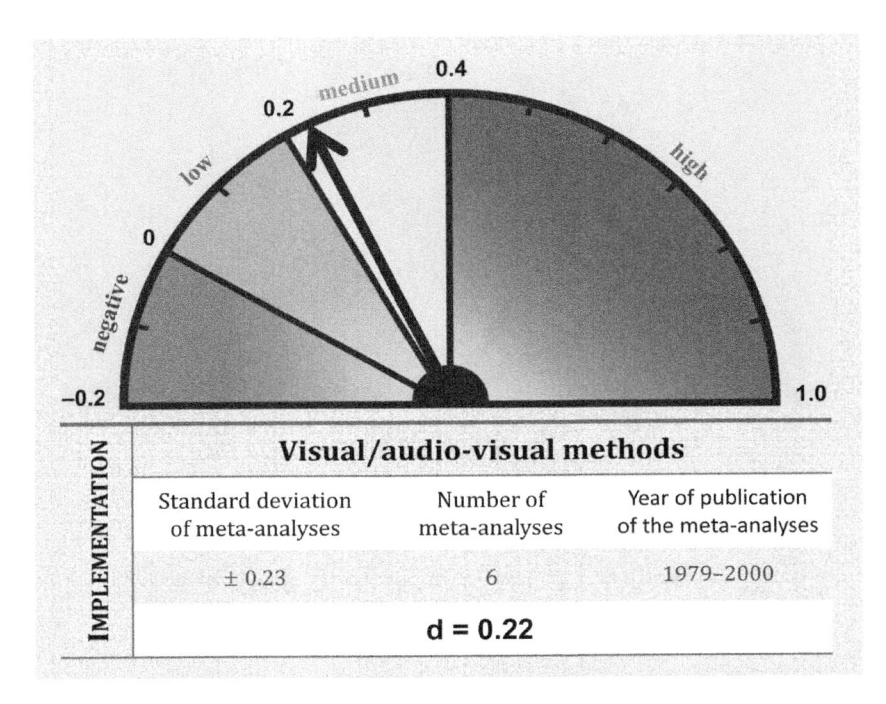

Figure 3.4 Factor "Visual/audio-visual methods"

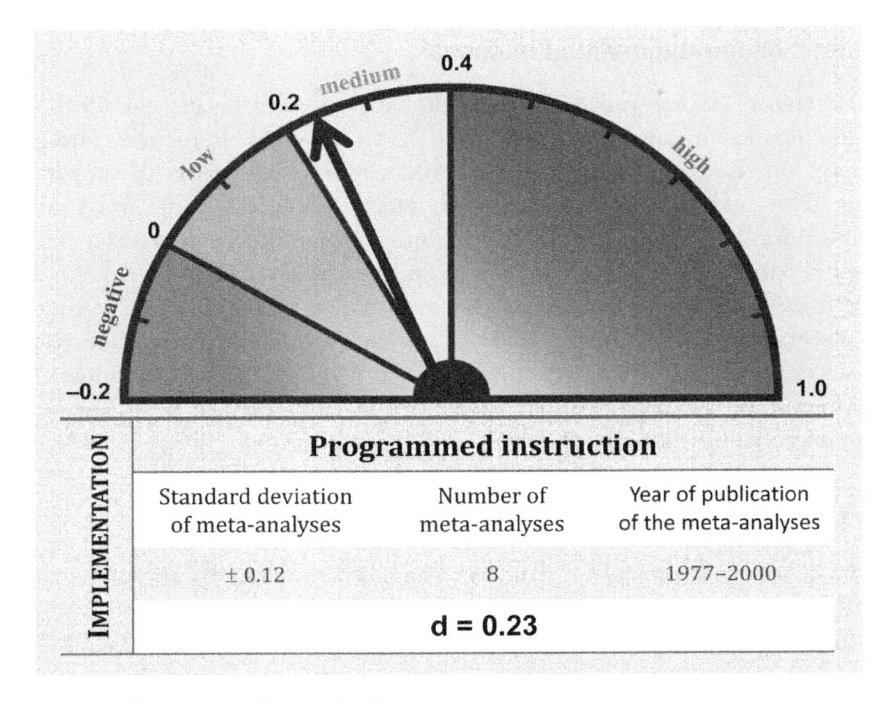

Figure 3.5 Factor "Programmed instruction"

thing to note with regard to digitalization in education is that replacing human communication with programmed instruction cannot be a successful strategy because it leaves the all-important phases of exchange, dialogue, and cooperation out of the learning process.

The factor "Use of calculators"

When the first pocket calculators arrived on the market with the promise of changing or possibly even revolutionizing mathematics teaching, there were big discussions with positions ranging from euphoric to apocalyptic—much like the more recent discussions on digitalization in education. In retrospect, the skeptics can claim that they were right: An effect size of 0.27 remains well below the bar of 0.4. It is worth taking a detailed look at the data, however, because it turns out that calculators can indeed serve their intended purpose. This is the case, for instance, when they reduce the cognitive strain on learners, allowing them to devote more effort to the actual problem and then to solve it, or when they are used as a means of checking one's own work for errors. There is evidence that these two uses together lead to a more positive attitude toward mathematics. As a simple replacement for arithmetical, logical, and spatial thinking, on the other hand, the use of calculators is problematic.

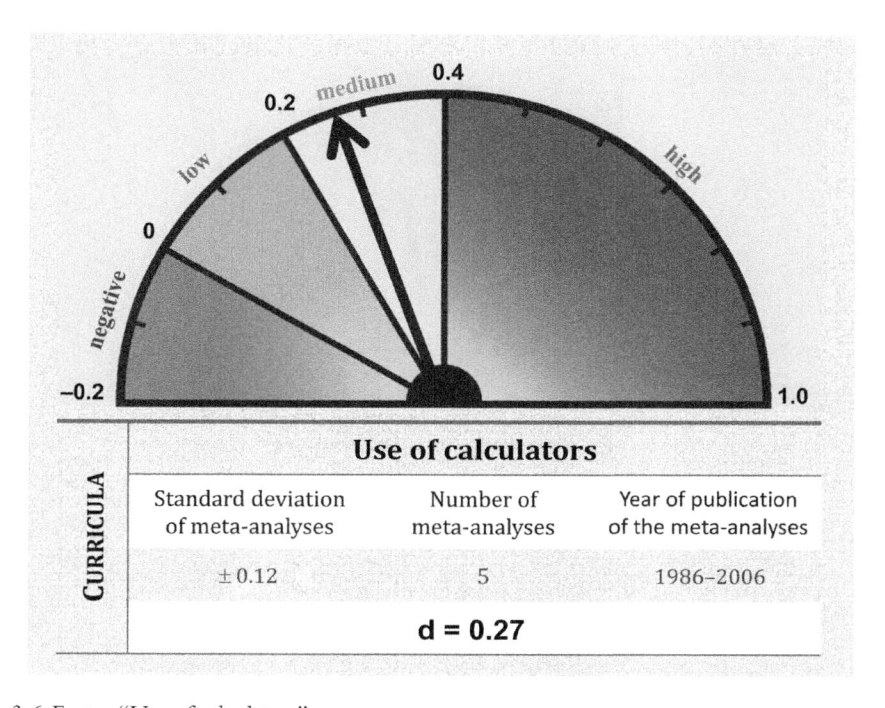

Use of calculators		
Standard deviation of meta-analyses	Number of meta-analyses	Year of publication of the meta-analyses
±0.12	5	1986–2006
d = 0.27		

Figure 3.6 Factor "Use of calculators"

The factor "Computer-assisted instruction"

The question of how computers can revolutionize learning in the classroom is one of the most frequent topics of educational meta-analyses. Nearly 40 of them have dealt with this topic in the last 40 years. That makes the use of computers—if one is to believe the dataset in Visible Learning—one of the best-studied domains of instructional research. The findings should therefore not be regarded merely as sound but also as important for future developments in this domain and particularly for the process of digitalization. This applies all the more in view of the effect size of 0.47, a result which, even though it is above the bar of 0.4, is dissappointing for many in the education sector. A great deal is expected of a computer revolution in the classroom, and the hopes are high. Why, then, does a use of computers not (yet) lead to larger effects? An initial observation from the primary studies is that computers are often used merely as a replacement for traditional media: The computer serves as a replacement for an encyclopedia, for worksheets, for a notebook, and so on and so forth. But it turns out that as long as computers are used only at this level, as a replacement for traditional media, they will not have a decisive impact. For in this case they serve like these traditional media only as a carrier of information. They will only be able to unfold their full potential—as may be seen in the meta-analyses and illustrated on the basis of their high standard deviation—to the extent that they are not used only for storing information but also for processing information. This information

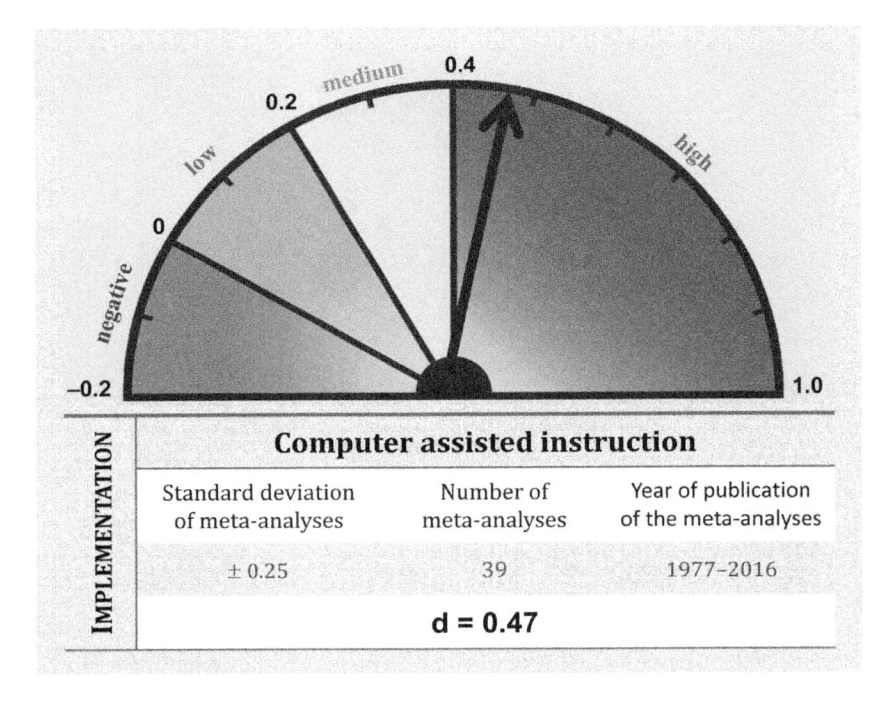

IMPLEMENTATION	Computer assisted instruction		
	Standard deviation of meta-analyses	Number of meta-analyses	Year of publication of the meta-analyses
	± 0.25	39	1977–2016
	d = 0.47		

Figure 3.7 Factor "Computer-assisted instruction"

processing is where computers may be assumed to have an advantage over other traditional media, because they enable an intensive exchange about learning, about mistakes, about strengths, and about weaknesses. Computers can therefore be used to initiate a dialogue and encourage cooperation.

The factor "One-on-one laptops"

Given the financial resources currently being pumped into the education system in support of digitalization, one of the measures implemented most frequently is to introduce laptop classes. The underlying idea is that if only every learner has his or her own laptop, then digital learning will simply happen on its own without requiring any further efforts. With an effect size of 0.16, however, the research findings on this factor point in a different direction and corroborate the main message arrived at in the discussion of the factor "computer–assisted instruction" above. This message is driven home with particular urgency in the previously mentioned study "The Pen Is Mightier Than the Keyboard" by Pam A. Mueller and Daniel M. Oppenheimer (2014). They succeeded in demonstrating that learners are better able to remember what they have heard when they take notes on paper than when they use a computer or laptop to do so. Hence, here too, it proves to be the case that technology alone has only little impact if it is not embedded in an overall pedagogical concept.

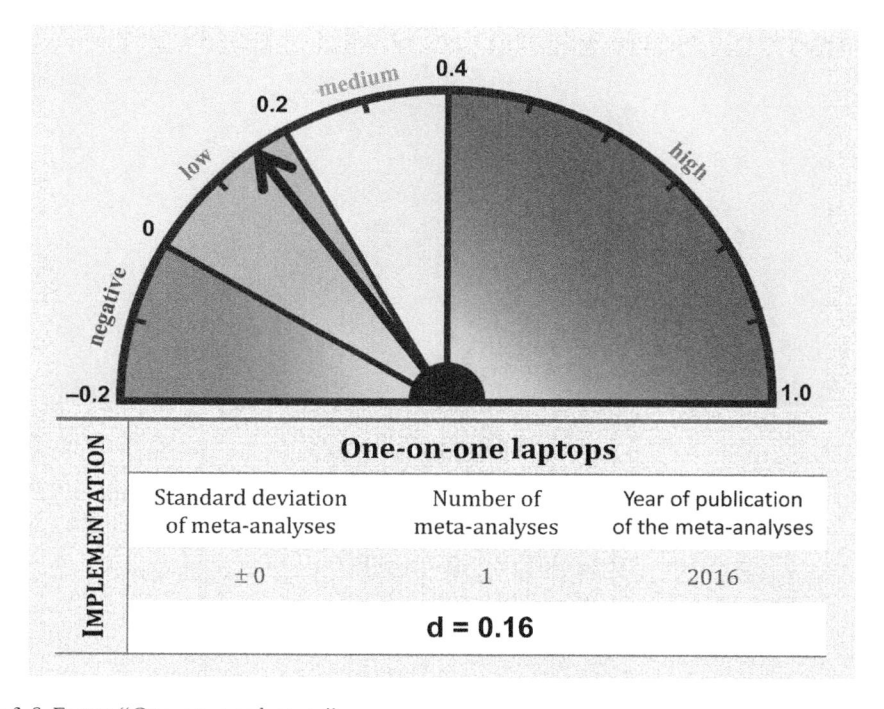

One-on-one laptops		
Standard deviation of meta-analyses	Number of meta-analyses	Year of publication of the meta-analyses
± 0	1	2016
d = 0.16		

Figure 3.8 Factor "One-on-one laptops"

The factor "Mobile phones"

The most influential mass medium today is doubtlessly the smartphone. Nearly every teenager has one, and it is even becoming more common to see them in the hands of younger children. The idea of using smartphones for instructional purposes seems only logical and has indeed been addressed increasingly by educational research in recent years. In Visible Learning, a total of four meta-analyses on this issue have been evaluated in the past ten years. Although the primary studies highlight a number of sensible possibilities for integrating smartphones into instruction, the effect size of 0.37 calculated for this factor remains below the bar of 0.4. Smartphones present opportunities for successful learning in that they can be used to access additional information that is helpful for subsequent pedagogical interactions. An example is obtaining feedback—whether formatively as feedback on a lesson or summatively as feedback on the learner's achievement level (cf. www.visiblefeedback.com and Zierer & Wisniewski, 2018). The teacher can easily take up this feedback and implement it in the next lesson. Despite these possibilities, however, it is also important to point out the limitations of smartphones in the classroom, which are divulged with special urgency in the study "Brain Drain" by Adrian F. Ward and colleagues (2017). They come to the conclusion that the mere presence of a smartphone leads to a loss of attentional resources and consequently to a reduction in performance.

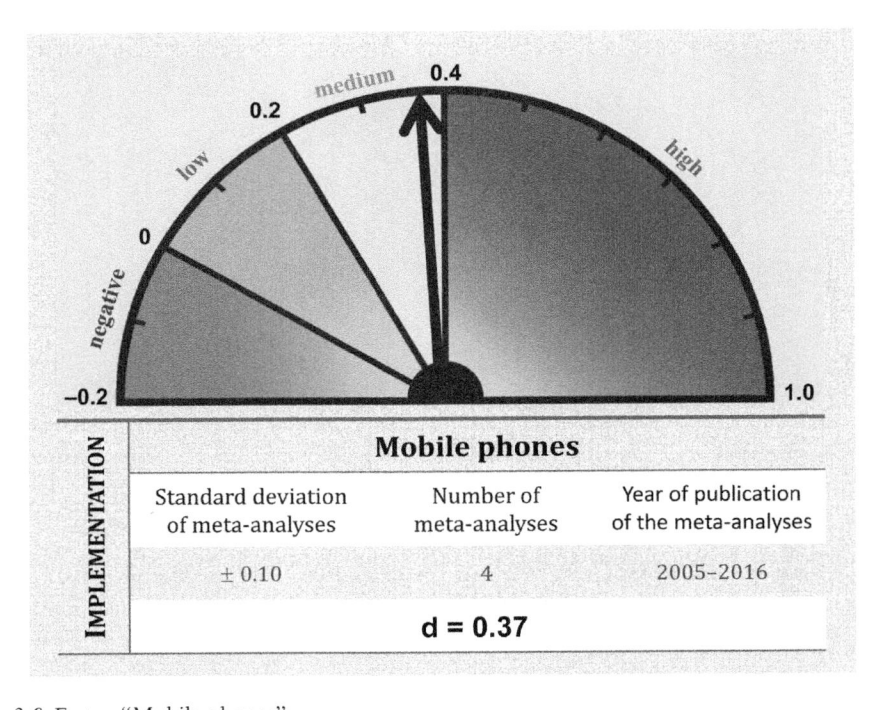

Mobile phones		
Standard deviation of meta-analyses	Number of meta-analyses	Year of publication of the meta-analyses
± 0.10	4	2005–2016
d = 0.37		

Figure 3.9 Factor "Mobile phones"

Attention and performance improve again only when when the smartphone is no longer located in the same room as the learner. Smartphones can therefore not just facilitate but also impede learning. Accordingly, smartphone use should be made into a central topic of media education.

The factor "Use of PowerPoint"

One would be hard pressed to find a medium that has done as much to change the way we communicate knowledge and pass on information in all social spheres as PowerPoint. The slideshows are virtually ubiquitous in meetings, conferences, lectures, and seminars—and as everybody knows, the exception proves the rule. Apple founder Steve Jobs, for instance, doubtlessly attached great importance to digitalization. Yet he of all people did not allow PowerPoint presentations in his meetings. It was his conviction that people who know what they're talking about don't need PowerPoint to get their ideas across. A glance at Visible Learning proves him right, because use of PowerPoint achieves an effect size of only 0.26. Numerous primary studies propose reasons why the use of PowerPoint has only little or even negative effects on learners. First of all, studies show that listeners often follow the slides rather than the speaker. As a result, what they are seeing takes the place of what they are hearing, meaning that technology replaces the

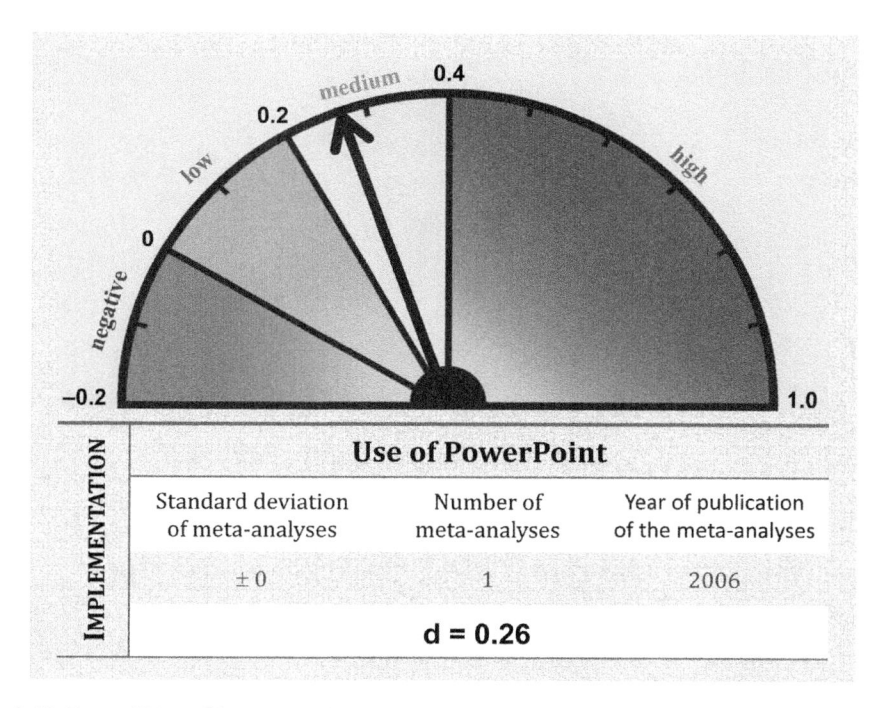

Figure 3.10 Factor "Use of PowerPoint"

speaker. Second, they show that speakers often speak more quickly and less convincingly when using PowerPoint. And third, they point out that slides are often weighed down with too much information. That is not just to say that they have too much text but also that the illustrations presented on them are not drawn successively (as would necessarily be the case on a blackboard) but rather appear all at once. All of this can hinder learning, if not prevent it altogether. To take advantage of the educational possibilities offered by PowerPoint, we therefore need teachers who are sufficiently professional to know the limitations of this medium.

The factor "Interactive video methods"

In contrast to all of the other factors described above, "interactive video methods" exceeds the bar of 0.4, with an overall effect size of 0.54 from six meta-analyses. It should be noted, however, that the effects of this factor vary slightly. This variation may be attributed primarily to the topic, the way in which it is prepared, and the possibility of self-regulation. For example, a combination of sounds and images or animations is more effective than purely verbal explanations, and colorful representations have advantages over black-and-white representations. Another key criterion is that learning videos should not only be designed for individual use but should also include individual feedback. Exchange and cooperation therefore play a central role here as well.

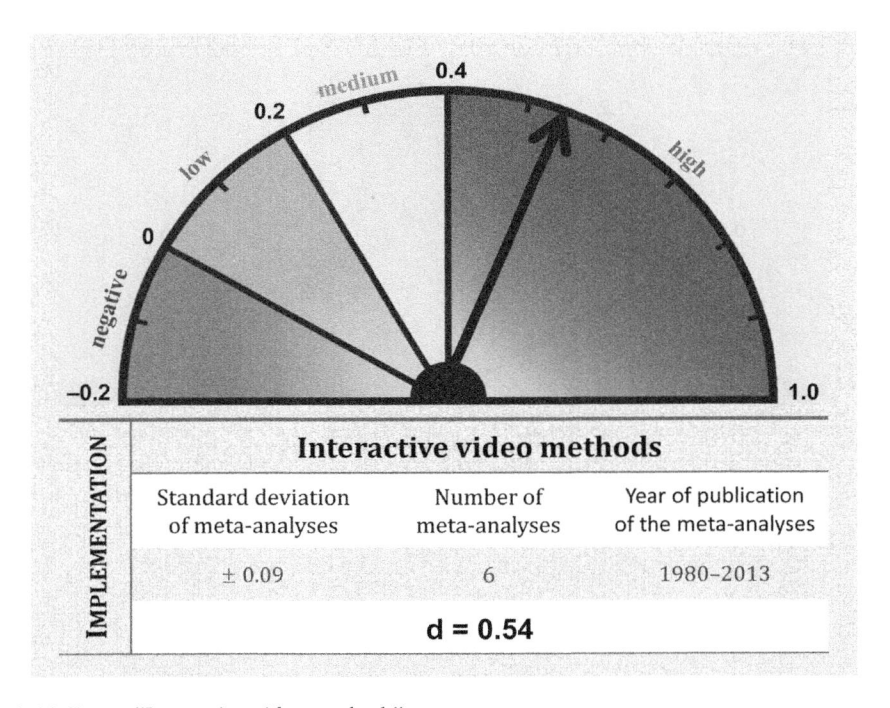

Figure 3.11 Factor "Interactive video methods"

The factor "Intelligent tutoring system"

At first glance, this factor seems to demonstrate how successful digitalization can be in education. After all, intelligent tutoring systems achieve an effect size of 0.48 in Visible Learning. However, a closer look reveals that the standard deviation of the meta-analyses is quite large at 0.13, meaning that effect sizes lower than 0.40 are possible. What does this factor involve, and how can its effects be explained? Intelligent tutoring systems are computer programs pioneered by researchers such as Derek H. Sleeman and James R. Hartley that formulate questions of various levels of difficulty in particular knowledge domains for learners to answer depending on their achievement level. An intelligent tutoring system is capable, on the basis of the answer provided, of either providing appropriate support to the learner or asking another question that is closer to that learner's learning level. Intelligent tutoring software that can be programmed and effectively integrated into instruction is available for specific subjects, such as mathematics, physics, chemistry, or vocabulary training for foreign languages. The easier to define and the more straightforward the content of a domain is, the better it can be conveyed in an intelligent tutoring system. At the same time, however, this aspect reveals the limitations of this method: Not every subject has content that can be conveyed in a computer program, and not every level of challenge can be packaged as a software solution. Subjects like theology, philosophy, or political science, for instance, are less suitable, because they are focused more on meaning and demand a level of comprehension that does not

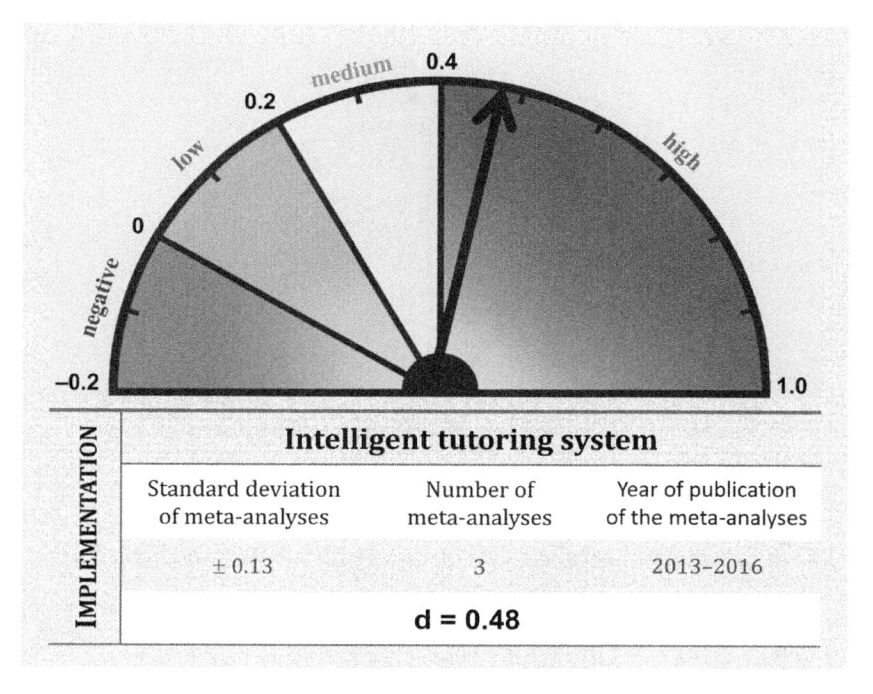

Figure 3.12 Factor "Intelligent tutoring system"

lend itself to clearly definable and straightforward response formats. Consequently, an intelligent tutoring system reaches its limits with tasks that demand more than the simple conveyance of knowledge in the form of reproduction and reorganization and can offer only little support in the domains of transfer and problem solving. Whether an intelligent tutoring system can achieve a positive effect thus depends on the teacher's ability to decide on the basis of a well-founded diagnosis of the students' achievement levels when a tool of this kind is appropriate. The consideration of motivational and also emotional aspects plays a special role in this decision, because they are not (yet) identified in intelligent tutoring systems.

The factor "Technology with learning-needs students"

The factor "technology with learning-needs students" attains a respectable effect size of 0.57. The reasons for this are immediately clear—and are perhaps particularly suitable for demonstrating the benefits digital learning has to offer: Technical advances can help students with special learning needs to access things that were previously inaccessible for them. One need only think of technologies for visualizing auditory information for the deaf or for converting images into spoken language for the blind. For these learners, digitalization provides new possibilities for participating in the classroom. Moreover, this factor also includes intervention programs designed primarily to support learning-needs students with knowledge acquisition and hence with learning at the levels of reproduction and reorganization. This may

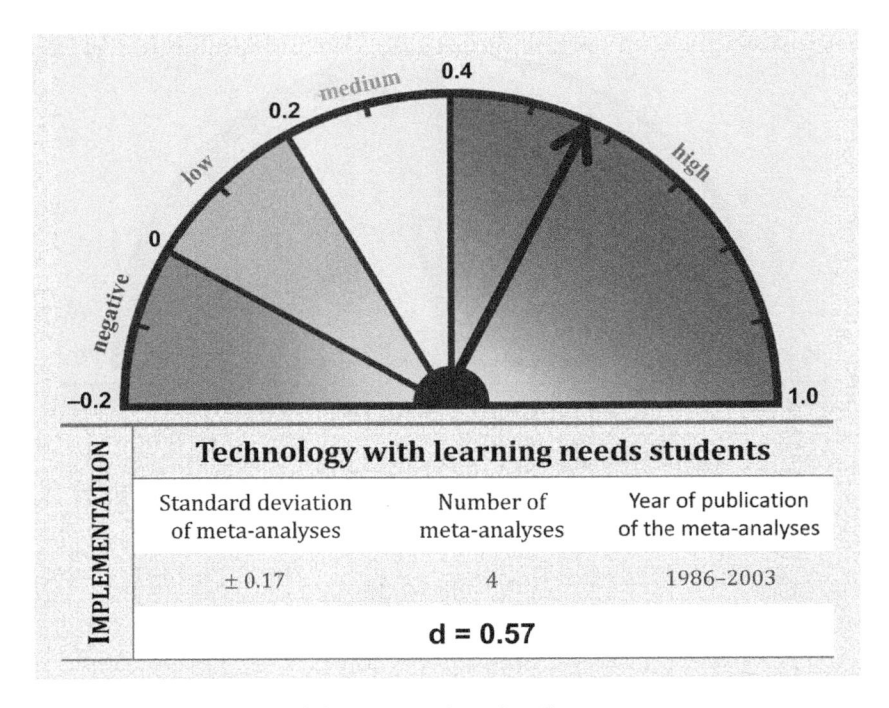

Figure 3.13 Factor "Technology with learning-needs students"

again also be realized with the help of technical methods, such as those described in connection with the factor "intelligent tutoring systems."

Conclusion: Learning is still learning

So what is the upshot of the empirical studies on the effectiveness of school interventions in the context of digitalization? What conclusions do they allow us to draw? It is worth it to first take another look at the factors discussed above and their average overall effect sizes, shown in Table 3.2.

Altogether, they achieve an average effect size of 0.33. One is therefore inclined to believe that the digital revolution we have been waiting 30 to 40 years for will not come to pass in this form.

Table 3.2 Effects of digitalization factors

Factor	Effect size
Clicker	0.22
Computer-assisted instruction	0.47
Technology in distance education	0.01
Technology in mathematics	0.33
Technology in other subjects	0.55
Technology in reading/literacy	0.29
Technology in science	0.23
Technology in small groups	0.21
Technology in writing	0.42
Technology with college students	0.42
Technology with elementary students	0.44
Technology with high school students	0.30
Technology with learning-needs students	0.57
Interactive video methods	0.54
Intelligent tutoring system	0.48
Mobile phones	0.37
Use of calculators	0.27
Programmed instruction	0.23
Use of PowerPoint	0.26
Visual/audio-visual methods	0.22
Web-based learning	0.18
Gaming/simulation	0.35
Online, digital tools	0.29
One-on-one laptops	0.16
Average	**0.33**

What is more important than the effect sizes of these factors, however, is how they came about. Only if we understand why a factor does not achieve the hoped-for effect is it possible to develop support measures to perhaps allow this effect to be achieved in the future. Why, then, is digitalization not (yet) capable of exerting a greater influence on the performance of learners in school? The reasons have already been touched on above, but I will present them once again in concentrated form in the following.

The mere act of setting up the newest technology in the classroom will not lead teachers to integrate it into their lessons in a meaningful way and to fully exploit the undeniable potential of digitalization. Rather, they will use new media primarily as a replacement for traditional media and thus exclusively as a carrier of information: The computer as a replacement for an encyclopedia, the tablet as a replacement for worksheets, and the interactive whiteboard as a replacement for a blackboard. However, an important finding of numerous primary studies in this domain is that it is not difficult for teachers to achieve effect sizes higher than the average of $d = 0.4$ if they succeed in using new media not just to store information but also to process information. An example of such a use of new media might be a physical education teacher who records the movement patterns of a student on video and then discusses them with her, watching the video with her backwards and forwards and in slow motion, thus instigating cognitive processes that would not be possible with traditional media.

To sum up, it follows that digitalization can be helpful in the classroom if it is not an end in itself but rather:

- takes into account the learner's current level of achievement;
- presents a challenge;
- builds confidence and enables trust;
- makes mistakes visible; and
- initiates discussions on the learner's own learning process.

By following these principles for digitalization in education, teachers can take the step from using digital technologies for storing information to using them for processing information. In this way, digitalization can engender more cognitive and social connectivity. If they fail to follow these principles, however, digitalization will remain at the level of a replacement for traditional media and will not have any lasting positive effects on student learning.

Several problematic messages surrounding digitalization in education emerge at this point. A view one commonly comes across, for instance, a claim also made by many a technology company, is that learning is easy if you only have the right technology at your disposal. Nothing could be further from the truth, because learning always involves effort. Learning means pushing your limits, admitting it when you cannot do something, putting in the effort and showing the dedication to develop yourself, and it also means making mistakes, taking detours, and taking wrong turns. Education always involves changes, and the question it provides an answer to is not what someone else made out of me but what I made out of my own life (cf. Zierer, 2015a).

Neil Postman (1985) argues in a similar vein. He warns against seeing instruction as entertainment in light of an increasing use of technology in the education sector: Good entertainment sets no challenge, demands no effort, and is not binding. Good instruction is precisely the opposite: It sets the challenge, demands effort, and is based on the reciprocal rights and duties of learners and the teacher.

This point loses nothing of its importance even if we speak of the generation growing up today as digital natives, as explained in the first chapter. It might very well be that today's children and youths are growing up with a different awareness for new media, but that changes nothing about the fact that they learn according to the same principles as the generations that came before them: They need clear goals, structured learning environments, phases of deliberate practice, and an intensive teacher–student relationship. Human evolution cannot keep pace with the digital revolution in this case. Learning is therefore still learning—whether it is digital or not. This notion can be illustrated by means of the forgetting curve in Figure 3.14 (cf. Hattie & Zierer, 2017, p. 64).

Psychological research demonstrates that we need to review information at least six to eight times to transfer it from short-term memory to long-term memory. If we fail to review information we have learned, forgetting takes its course. In other words, we begin to forget things as soon as we have learned them. This principle applies regardless of the media one used to learn the information.

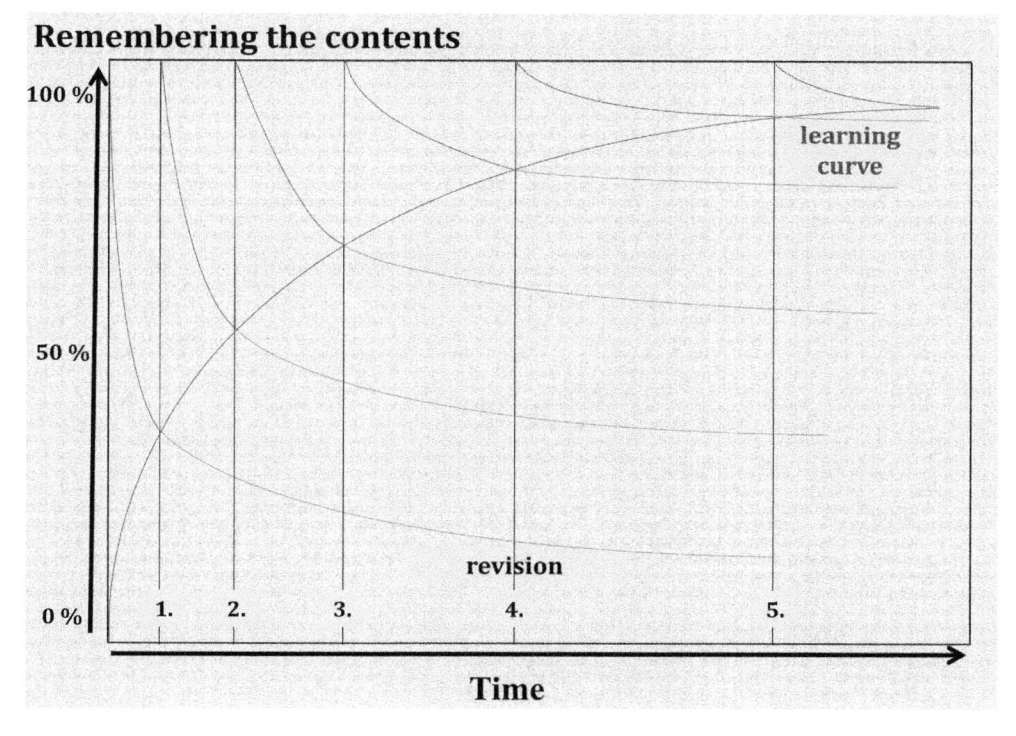

Figure 3.14 Forgetting curve

Hence, in order to reap the additional benefits that digitalization does in fact offer over and above those of traditional media, it is necessary to take the step from storing information to processing information. Since this will only succeed if teachers are capable of taking this step, they need to be offered systematic professional development measures—which, incidentally, achieve an effect size of $d = 0.51$ (Hattie, 2014, p. 278; see also Hattie, 2013, pp. 143–145). These measures would need to make it clear to teachers what digitalization can be useful for and how to integrate it effectively into teaching and learning processes. Unfortunately, educational policymakers do not always think of offering such measures: They often invest in technology without investing in people and assume that every teacher who owns a mobile phone and a computer knows how to integrate this technology into their lessons in a meaningful way. This is not the case, as educational research demonstrates. This is another example of how structural changes are so often made without involving the people who can breathe life into these structural changes. The goal should be to establish structures and strengthen people.

New media enthusiasts willingly concede that these objections are perfectly justified but then go on to defend themselves by arguing that this is only true of hardware and software that is five to ten years old and that the latest advances of the computer age are already a step further and have overcome these deficiencies. Here too, however, the findings of empirical educational research tell a different tale: If, for instance, one takes up this objection and views the meta-analyses found by John Hattie for the factor "computer-assisted instruction" by year of publication and effect size, one obtains the graphical representation shown in Figure 3.15.

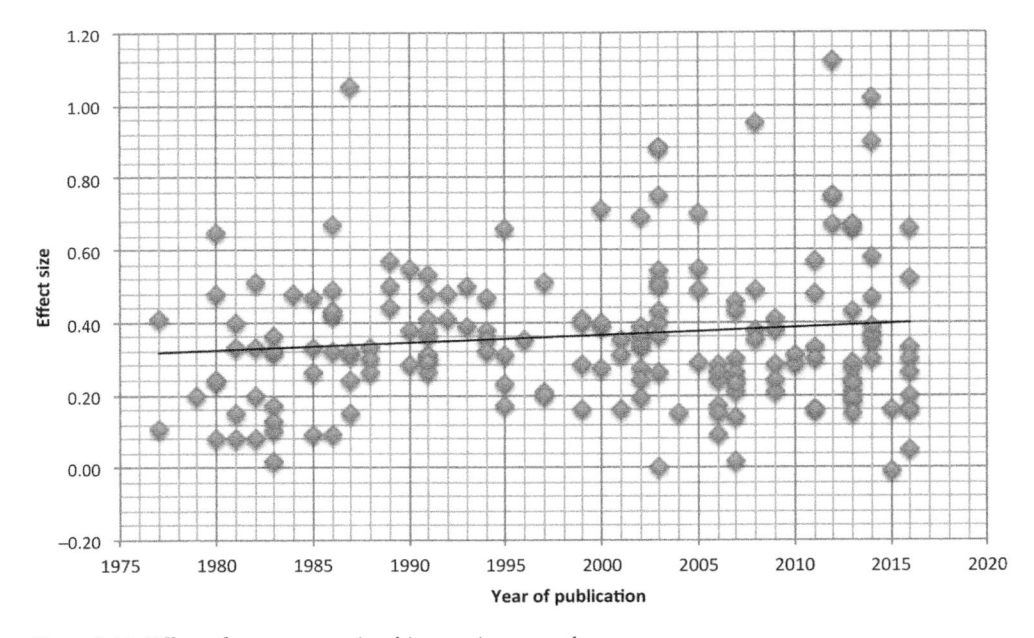

Figure 3.15 Effect of computer–assisted instruction over the years

Figure 3.15 shows (in addition to a high dispersion) a slight increase in effect sizes with the year of publication of the primary studies in the past 30, 40 years—which, however, does not reach the domain of desired effects. It is interesting to compare this increase with the more than rapid pace of technological advancements in the context of digitalization. Take, for instance, the development in the performance of processors and storage media. It must therefore be conceded that pedagogy has not kept up with digitalization. And yet how could it, given that learning is governed by other principles than digitalization. Even the latest breakthroughs of the digital age can change nothing about this—and it would be foolish to expect them to. The most advanced technology also needs people who can operate it correctly, and programmers are more prone than ever to take the increased programming possibilities open to them in questionable directions.

Hence, the success of digitalization in education hinges on the professionalism of the teachers.

Summary

WHAT PROCEDURE IS APPLIED IN VISIBLE LEARNING?

Visible Learning encompasses the largest dataset of empirical educational research ever to be analyzed in a single book. John Hattie collected more than 800 meta-analyses and combined them to form a synthesis. The result is 150 factors whose influence on student learning performance is measured by means of effect sizes. The effect size d = 0.4 plays a special role, marking the point at which pedagogical measures begin to achieve an above-average effect.

WHAT ARE THE GENERAL RESULTS REGARDING DIGITAL LEARNING?

The key to the success of a digital learning method is not the age of the learners, not the subject, and not the technology. Rather, the general results of Visible Learning indicate that what is more important is how well the teacher succeeds in integrating digital learning into a lesson.

WHAT EFFECT DO THE FACTORS "TECHNOLOGY WITH LEARNING-NEEDS STUDENTS," "INTERACTIVE VIDEO METHODS," "INTELLIGENT TUTORING SYSTEM," "COMPUTER-ASSISTED INSTRUCTION," "MOBILE PHONES," VISUAL/AUDIO-VISUAL METHODS," "USE OF CALCULATORS," "USE OF POWERPOINT," "PROGRAMMED INSTRUCTION," "WEB-BASED LEARNING," AND "ONE-ON-ONE LAPTOPS" HAVE ON LEARNING OUTCOMES?

Altogether, these factors remain below the bar of 0.4, achieving an average effect size of only 0.34. A more detailed look at the studies shows that individual factors can indeed break into the domain of desired effects. When this is the case, however, the reason is to be found less in the nature of the technology than in the competence and mind frames of the people working with this technology.

WHAT IS THE MAIN MESSAGE OF PREVIOUS RESEARCH ON DIGITALIZATION IN SCHOOL AND INSTRUCTION?

As important as it is to achieve digitalization in education, simply equipping schools with the latest technology will not spark a learning revolution. The key factor for the success of digitalization in education is the people who work with the technology. Particularly critical for this task are their competence and mind frames. As a consequence, educational policymakers should not just establish structures but also strengthen the people who can breathe life into these structures.

WHY IS LEARNING STILL LEARNING?

The notion that digitalization can revolutionize learning ignores the fact that learning does not follow the mechanisms of progress. Rather, it is subject to evolutionary processes that are far slower and more constant. It turns out that digitalization has no effect on certain principles of learning. To reiterate the example used above, research shows that we need to review information we have learned at least six to eight times to commit it to long-term memory.

4

From information storage to information processing

A model for orientation

Task for reflection

Reflect on what consequences the change from information storage to information processing must have with regard to digitalization. Can you think of examples of new media being used for a different purpose?

Goals

In this chapter you will learn about a model designed to support you in the classroom on a daily basis. It was originally developed by Ruben C. Puentedura and has been enhanced and refined to reflect the ideas presented so far in this book. When you finish reading this chapter, you should be able to answer the following questions:

- What was Ruben C. Puentedura's intention in developing the SAMR model?
- What characterizes digitalization at the levels of substitution, augmentation, modification, and redefinition?
- What was the intention in developing the iPAC framework?
- What characterizes digitalization from the point of view of the three principal constructs "personalization," "authenticity," and "collaboration"?
- How can the SAMR model and the iPAC framework be combined?
- Why is "why" the most important question to ask with regard to the use of media?

As reasonable as the main message of the last chapter may be, it does not go very far in providing teachers with concrete support. Teachers need to call upon their professionalism and decide anew in each individual class situation what medium to use, how to use it, and especially what purpose it is supposed to serve.

The field of general didactics—the science of learning and teaching at all grade levels, in all subjects, and at all types of schools—has set itself the task of offering teachers didactic models designed to serve as working models to help them meet the challenges involved in this endeavor.

Karl-Heinz Flechsig (1991) describes working models as being located between descriptions of practice and categorical models. Whereas the former describe a concrete situation and thus illustrate how one can do something, the latter formulate theoretical claims and thus show what would need to be present in order for something to work. Working models, on the other hand, are characterized by a practical theory or theoretical practice. They attempt to name epistemologically grounded and empirically validated generalizations for orientation purposes.

A model of this kind that is particularly worthy of mention in the context of digitalization is the SAMR model by Ruben C. Puentedura (cf. Puentedura, 2017a, 2017b; Common Sense, 2017; Wilke, 2017). Another model of this kind that is particularly worthy of mention in the context of digitalization is the iPAC framework, developed by a group of researchers and teacher educators from the University of Hull, United Kingdom and the University of Technology, Sydney, Australia (cf. Kearney, Schuck, Burden & Aubusson, 2012; Mobilelearningtoolkit, 2018). Both are famous in the field of digitalization and both meet the criteria for a working model described above and can therefore serve as the basis for the following discussion.

The SAMR model

In essence, the SAMR model differentiates between four levels of digitalization in school and instruction:

1   At the level of substitution, digitalization serves as a substitute for traditional media. It does not lead to any additional benefits, nor is it expected to do so.

2   At the level of augmentation, digitalization is understood as an extension of traditional media. It may lead to additional benefits, due to the fact that it can involve a combination of several different kinds of traditional media and because digital connectivity can improve speed and availability.

3   At the level of modification, digitalization is used to modify tasks in a way that would not be possible with traditional media.

4   At the level of redefinition, the task is redefined with regard to social and cognitive connectivity.

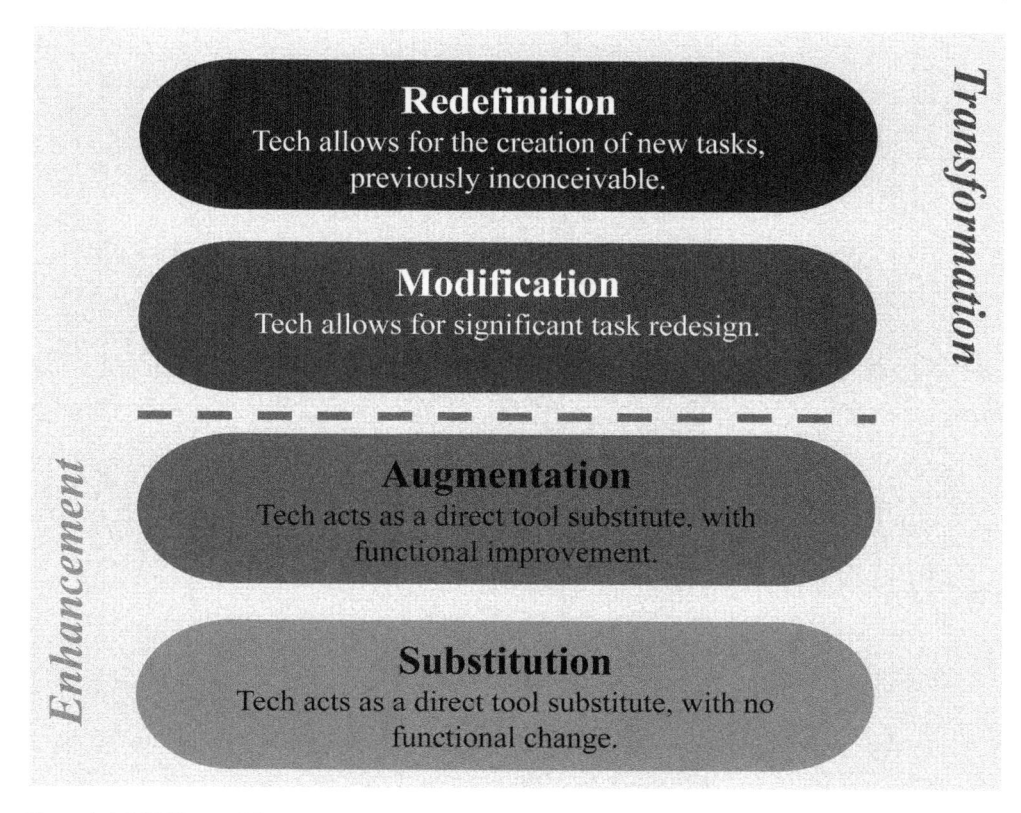

Figure 4.1 SAMR model

Source: cf. Common Sense (2017)

This brief description of levels of digitalization shows clearly where the transition from information storage to information processing is located. It takes place primarily between the second and the third level. If we apply this notion to John Hattie's principle of taking evidence as a basis for assessing learning outcomes, we may argue that the first and second levels of digitalization, where new media are seen as mere substitutes for their traditional counterparts, should produce an effect size of lower than 0.4. Digitalization becomes more interesting at the third and fourth levels, where it should be possible to achieve effect sizes above 0.4.

This provides a basis for delineating the key realms of possibility for digitalization in school and instruction: The better teachers succeed at integrating new media into their lessons in such a way that tasks are modified and redefined with regard to the level of challenge and the degree of communication, the more influence they will have on the learning performance of their students.

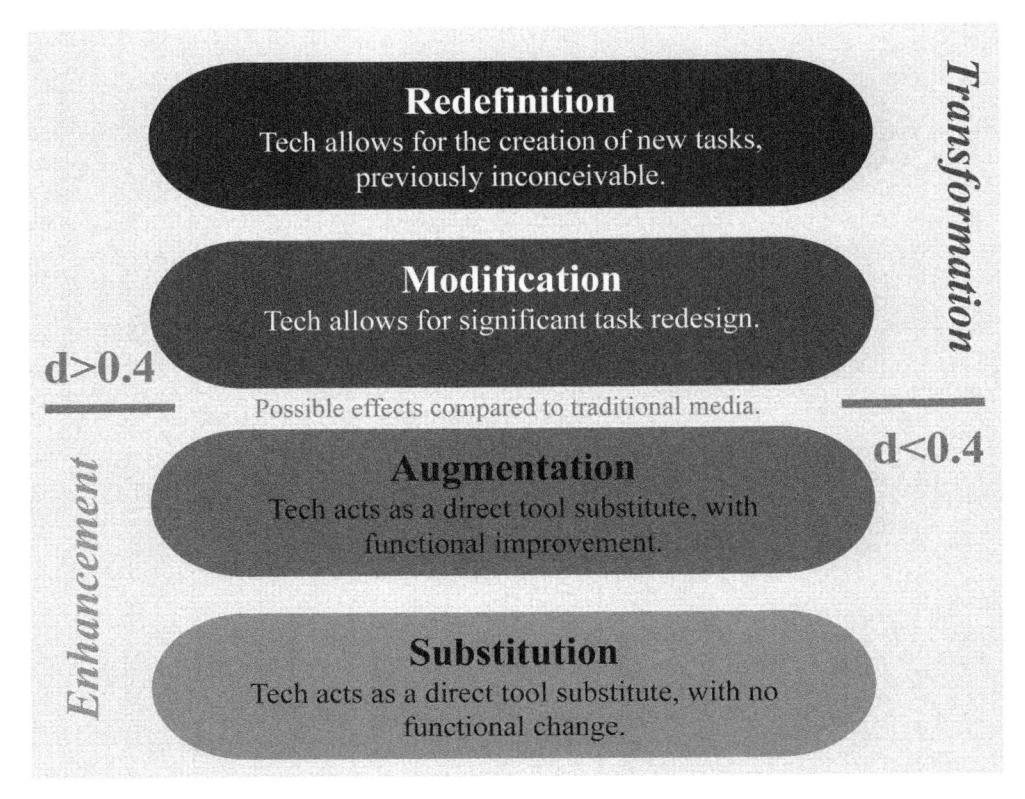

Figure 4.2 SAMR model and effect size

Source: cf. Common Sense (2017)

What is also interesting about this model is how it is linked to the definition of learning 4.0 as formulated above, namely as a form of learning that is marked first by a high degree of cognitive connectivity and second by a high degree of social connectivity. Learning 4.0 therefore corresponds in nature to the level of redefinition described by Ruben C. Puentedura. Furthermore, learning 1.0 may be regarded as a form of learning located at the level of substitution, exhibiting little cognitive and social connectivity. The higher the degree of connectivity is in these fields, the higher is the likelihood that a transition to learning 2.0 and learning 3.0 will occur.

The important point in this connection is the insight that digitalization is not the only way to achieve a learning 4.0 as defined in this way. Learning does not necessarily need digitalization to achieve a high degree of cognitive connectivity on the one hand and a high degree of social connectivity on the other. Rather, the relationship in this context is the other way around: The domain of high cognitive and social connectivity is where digitalization has the most possibilities. Hence, the additional benefits open to digitalization lies in penetrating into just this domain.

I will go into each of these levels in more detail in the following sections, taking the task of writing a story as an example. The reason for choosing this example is that it is an everyday classroom assignment that can be done in one's native language or in a foreign language.

The level of substitution

School students typically use paper and pencil to write their stories and complete the assignment to the best of their ability. Asking them to use a computer instead of paper and pencil to write their stories introduces digitalization to the learning process, but this digitalization occurs exclusively at the level of substitution: The computer serves merely as a substitute for paper and pencil. It will not be possible to achieve any additional learning benefits in this way. The story will not be different just because it is written on a computer. If the learners cannot type as fast as they can write by hand, there is even the danger that substituting traditional media with new media will lead to a negative effect. This is thus another example of how digitalization can also hinder learning. As a consequence, the key question will be that of "why": What goal are we trying to reach in applying new media?

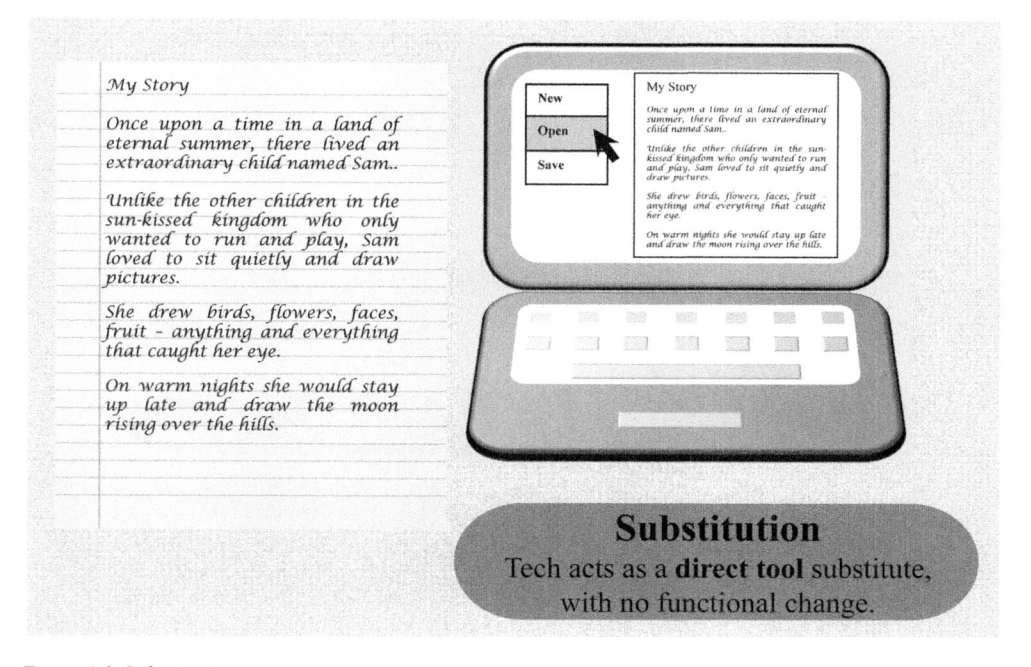

Figure 4.3 Substitution

Source: cf. Common Sense (2017)

Illustration created using the © PF–Images page, fotolia.com

The level of augmentation

In addition to paper and pencil, the learners can also be provided with various reference works to help them with their assignment of writing a story, for instance a dictionary, a grammar book, or a style guide. While these aids will not necessarily enhance the content of the story, they can be a big help with regard to the language. Digitalization would be easy to realize in this case, since nearly all word processors feature an integrated spellchecker, grammar checker, and style guide. Since these functions are generally very quick and convenient to use and are also connected with one another, the use of a computer can serve in this case not just as a substitute for traditional media but also as an augmentation of these media. A higher degree of cognitive connectivity is therefore possible.

However, it is important to point out that negative effects in comparison to traditional media can creep into the learning process at the level of augmentation as well. This has to do with the possibilities of programming the software—we all know what it's like when the computer does not do things the way we wish it would and we could have completed a task more quickly without it. Weighed down by optical and acoustic effects, a flash here and a whiz there, quite a few programs lead to "cognitive overload" (cf. Chandler &

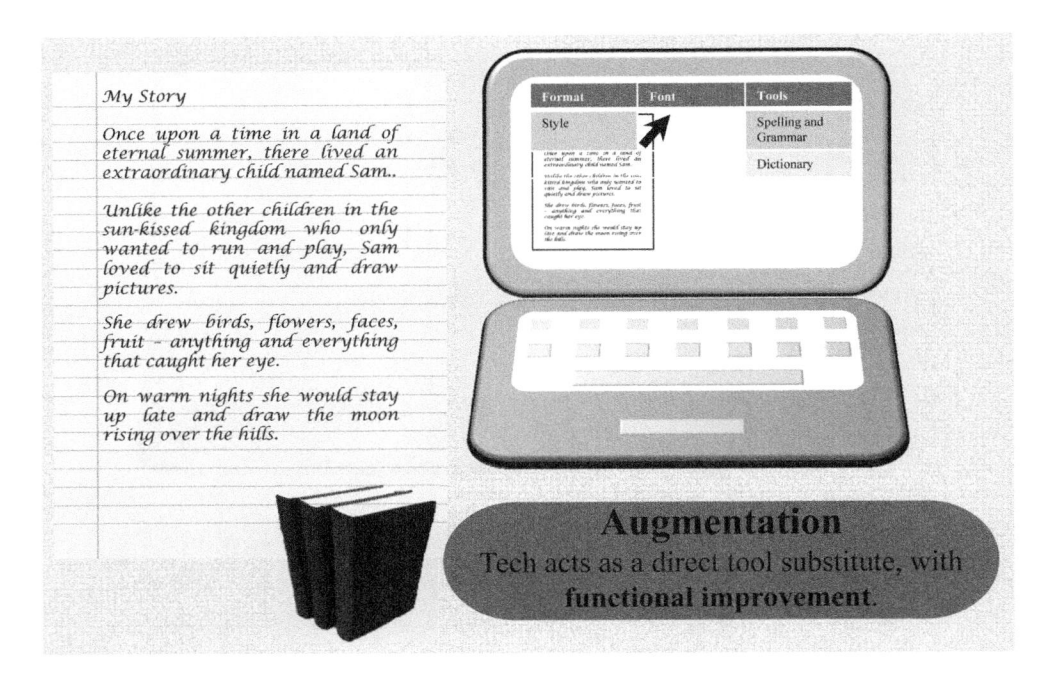

Figure 4.4 Augmentation

Source: cf. Common Sense (2017)

Illustration created using the © PF–Images page, fotolia.com

Sweller, 1991) and thus to an unnecesary strain on working memory. Children and youths who work with these programs often expend a large part of their cognitive capacity sorting out and selecting from the various stimuli rather than working on the task at hand—and rather than learning. Hence, too many possibilities can place an unnecessary strain on working memory. Digitalization can hinder learning.

The level of modification

It is possible to modify the task in our example with the help of digitalization if the learners do not just have the assignment of writing a story but of writing it in a team. This is very difficult with paper and pencil: The learners need to be in the same place at the same time, and even then only one of them can write at once. New media open up the possibility of working on one and the same text from different places and at different times. Every member of the team can contribute, everyone can follow the changes, accept them or reject them, and comment on them. It should be stressed that all of this is also possible without digitalization, but it is quicker and easier to do with digitalization. The result is therefore a higher degree of social connectivity.

Figure 4.5 Modification

Source: cf. Common Sense (2017)

Illustration created using the pointing hand © Bitter, fotolia.com

The level of redefinition

If we take the level of modification in the above example one step further, we might say that the team's assignment is not just to write a story but also to write a screenplay for it in which every member of the team has a role, and that they then have to make a video based on this screenplay. This redefinition of the task results initially in a stronger cognitive connectivity, because it is no longer just about writing a story but about making a film. The learners could then be asked to digitally edit the film and load it onto a communication platform, enabling an exchange beyond the immediate classroom environment. This might be a partner class in another country, for example, that could react directly to the film or even add their own scenes. Hence, this redefinition through digital means would also result in a stronger social connectivity, making it an example of learning 4.0. It should be clear that the additional benefits offered by digitalization in this constellation is not possible at all with traditional media or would at least involve great effort and a lot of time to organize.

Figure 4.6 Redefinition

Source: cf. Common Sense (2017)

Illustration created using figures © Christine Wulf and easel © djdarkflower

An important qualification should be mentioned with regard to the levels of modification and redefinition as well. Here again, misconceived and misdirected digitalization can lead, if not to negative effects, then at least to unnecessarily lower effects: The social connectivity described at these levels is only beneficial as long as it does not function as a substitute for traditional forms of communication and cooperation. If, for instance, exchange on an online forum serves as a substitute for personal communication that would be equally feasible to organize, then digitalization loses its advantage over traditional media. In fact, it reverts from the initially possible level of redefinition all the way back to the level of substitution, which causes any positive effect not only to disappear but possibly also to turn into a negative effect. And yet it would seem obvious that nothing can replace the immediacy and directness of a personal discussion. Plato, it is worth recalling, stressed repeatedly that a dialogue is the best possible way for people to get into a discussion with one another.

The iPAC framework

Because a lot of theories which are used to explain and understand digital learning were not designed with mobile technologies specifically in mind, a group of researchers and teacher educators from the University of Hull, United Kingdom, and the University of Technology, Sydney, Australia set about investigating the unique and distinctive affordances of digital technologies. As a result Matthew Kearney, Sandra Schuck, Kevin Burden, and Peter Aubusson published for the first time in 2012 the core idea of the iPAC framework. With it the authors identify the specific pedagogical features or affordances of digital devices that make learning distinctive. These are referred to as the "signature pedagogies of mobile learning" and consist of three principal constructs: personalization, authenticity, and collaboration. Figure 4.7 illustrates this idea (cf. Kearney, Schuck, Burden & Aubusson, 2012; Mobilelearningtoolkit, 2018).

Before the iPAC framework is presented below, the following note: It is quite remarkable that the reception of the model concentrates almost without exception on these three principal constructs. In this way, the center is often lost from view: space and time. These two constants or boundaries traditionally characterize learning (cf. Kearney, Schuck, Burden & Aubusson, 2012): First, learning places occupy fixed, physical spaces which are defined by relatively impermeable boundary objects such as walls, classrooms and school buildings. Second, learning is situated in permanent temporal slots such as teaching periods which are relatively immutable. But digital learning has the potential to transcend these spatial and temporal restrictions: In spatial terms, digital learning is not fixed and offers a variety of alternatives (including virtual or non-geographical spaces). In temporal terms, digital learning does not require fixed, scheduled time spaces (which characterize current schooling) and it enables the individuals to be more flexible about when they learn. Bridging space and time

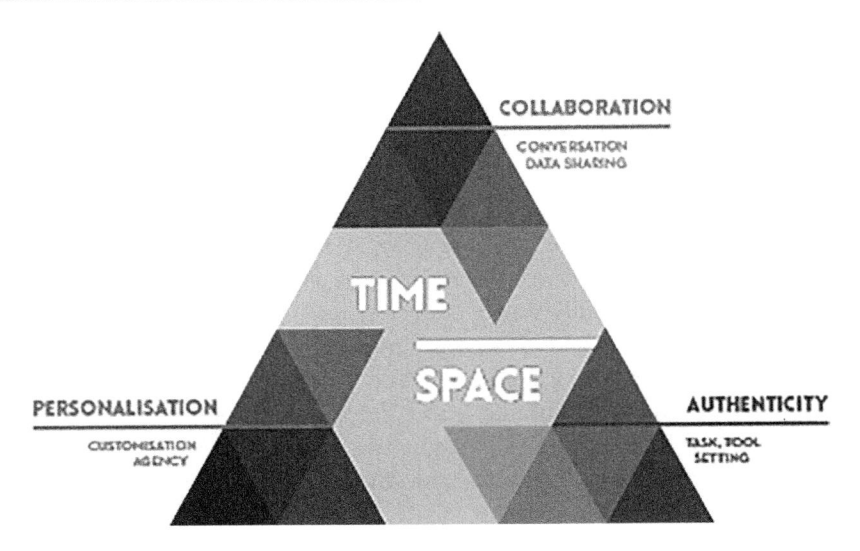

Figure 4.7 iPAC framework

Source: Kearney, M., Schuck, S., Burden, K., & Aubusson, P. (2012). Viewing mobile learning from a pedagogical perspective. *Research in Learning Technology* 20: 14406. doi: 10.3402/rlt.v20i0/14406

is without doubt a unique selling point and perhaps even the greatest advantage of digital learning. The iPAC framework sets this aspect at its center—thus it is worthwhile to mention it.

In the following sections I will discuss the three principal constructs in more detail, taking the task of creating an ebook as an example. The reason for choosing this example is that it is an everyday classroom assignment that can be done in one's native language or in a foreign language. Because the three principal constructs are broken down into seven operational sub-constructs, they will be described in more detail as well (cf. Mobilelearningtoolkit, 2018). These sub-constructs are important to understand if the iPAC framework is intended to be used as a planning and evaluative tool. Therefore a series of continuums is used to represent each of the seven sub-constructs, and for each of these there are two binary points which are described further below.

In doing this I try to show that the iPAC framework is helpful for making learning 4.0 visible as described above—and it is also helpful for showing that not all digital learning is per se effective.

The principal construct "personalization"

The principal construct "personalization" is widely recognized as a key benefit of digital learning. It includes pedagogical features such as learner choice, agency, and self-regulation, as well as customization. In well-designed digital learning activities, students have greater control over the place (physical or virtual), pace, and time they learn, and can enjoy autonomy over their learning content. Goals are typically set by learners and their peers. Furthermore, the learning experience can be customized for the individual learner. This can be at both the level of the tool and the activity. As a result, there are two sub-constructs: agency and customization. They extend from weak "external" to strong "internal" (agency), and from weak "one size fits all" to strong " individualized" (customization).

The principal construct "authenticity"

It is generally accepted that authentic tasks provide real-world relevance and personal meaning to the learner. Digital technologies support authentic learning through the setting, the task, and the tool. Settings can be both physical and virtual in the digital world, enabling learners to experience what it is like to learn on the spot. Task authenticity refers to the extent to which tasks are realistic and offer problems encountered by real-world practitioners. Tool authenticity relates to the apps and tools students are using and how far they replicate those of real-world practitioners. As a result, there are three sub-constructs: task, tool, and setting. They extend from weak "decontextualized" to strong "realistic" (task), from weak "artifical" to strong "practitioner-like" (tool), and from weak "contrived" to strong "realistic" (setting).

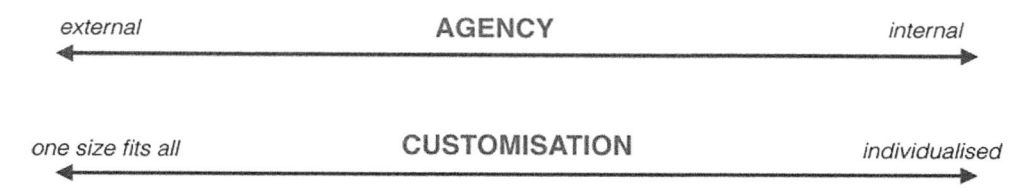

Figure 4.8 Personalization

Source: Kearney, M., Schuck, S., Burden, K., & Aubusson, P. (2012). Viewing mobile learning from a pedagogical perspective. *Research in Learning Technology* 20: 14406. doi: 10.3402/rlt.v20i0/14406

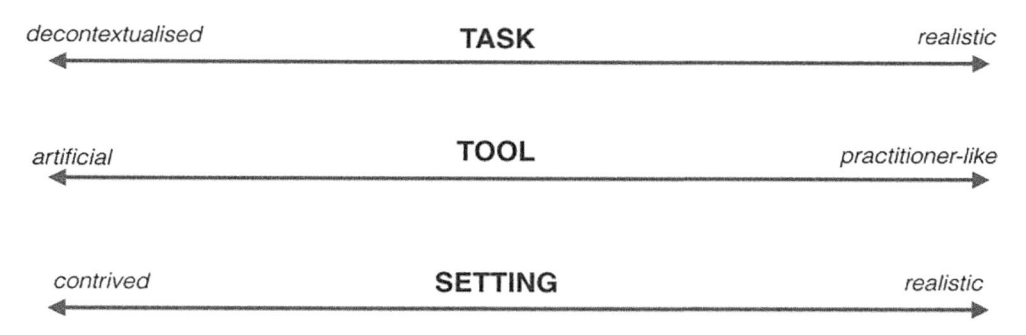

Figure 4.9 Authenticity

Source: Kearney, M., Schuck, S., Burden, K., & Aubusson, P. (2012). Viewing mobile learning from a pedagogical perspective. *Research in Learning Technology* 20: 14406. doi: 10.3402/rlt.v20i0/14406

The principal construct "collaboration"

Digital learning allows students to enjoy a high degree of collaboration by connecting peoples and their ideas mediated by a digital device. The networking capability of digital devices creates shared, socially interactive environments allowing learners to easily communicate multi-modally with peers, teachers, and other experts, and to exchange information. Learners consume, produce, and exchange an array of "content," sharing information and artifacts across time and space. As a result, there are two sub-constructs: conversation and data sharing. They reach from weak "solitary" to strong "networked" (conversation) and from weak "consumption" to strong "individualized" (production/sharing).

These are the three principal constructs and the seven sub-constructs, presented in binary codes reaching from weak to strong. This pattern is helpful for making learning 4.0 visible and for showing that not all digital learning is neither worthwhile nor effective.

An example: Students create an ebook

In a MTTE (Mobilising and Transforming Teacher Education Pedagogies) online course the following example is given (cf. Mobilelearningtoolkit, 2018): At Metis upper secondary school in Bergen, Norway, students created an ebook about the novel *The Great Gatsby*. Their ebook is based on a Great Gatsby project in the final-year English class (the students are 19 years old). First the students read the novel, second they worked in groups on the novel in class, third the students worked with teacher trainees, specializing in English at the University of Hull, United Kingdom, and last the students worked a full day with professional actors at West Yorkshire Playhouse in Leeds, United Kingdom, dramatizing parts of the novel. Based on all this experience they created their ebooks. The students are: Emma Lovise Fauskanger; Julie Tveit Pettersen, and Jenny Aase Bjørsvik.

This example shows the power of digital learning and the strong effects on the principal constructs: The digital learning setting is internal and individualized (personalization), realistic and practitioner-like (authenticity), as well as networked and productive (collaboration).

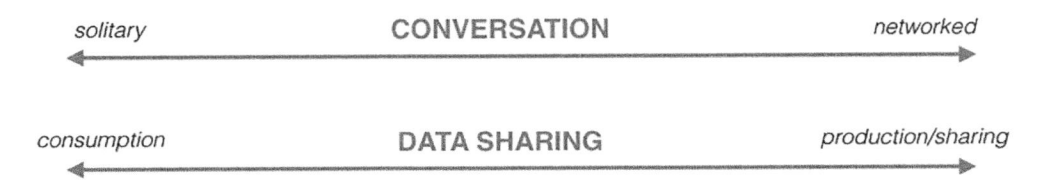

Figure 4.10 Collaboration

Source: Kearney, M., Schuck, S., Burden, K., & Aubusson, P. (2012). Viewing mobile learning from a pedagogical perspective. *Research in Learning Technology* 20: 14406. doi: 10.3402/rlt.v20i0/14406

Against this background Matthew Kearney, Sandra Schuck, Kevin Burden, and Peter Aubusson pointed out the following guideline for the iPAC framework in 2012:

1   The binary codes enable teachers to use the iPAC framework as an evaluative tool by assigning each sub-construct a score. So, for example, each sub-construct can be scored from weak to strong—distinguishing well-designed digital learning settings from poorly designed digital learning settings. In this way the iPAC framework can be used for a variety of different purposes which include:

   a)   to identify the current use of digital technologies in a specific teaching setting: e.g., after a lesson in which learners were asked to undertake a part or all of the lesson using their digital device;

   b)   as an evaluative tool to measure how teaching has changed over a period of time: e.g., measuring a lesson when you are a novice user of digital technologies and comparing this to a lesson in which you are becoming more of an expert;

   c)   as a tool to structure a reflective activity such as a conversation with a trainee teacher: e.g., both teacher and trainee teacher using the framework to score a lesson in which digital technologies were used and then exchanging scores and comparing the results;

   d)   as a planning tool to design a specific pedagogical activity using digital technologies: e.g., designing a lesson which made learning more authentic by encouraging learners to use their digital device as a tool in the way professionals might use it.

With the help of three further examples I want to illustrate these thoughts (cf. Kearney, Schuck, Burden & Aubusson, 2012):

1   Use of Twitter at conference: Delegates use Twitter at a professional learning conference. During keynote presentations, delegates tweeted brief comments and questions in reaction to the speakers (or other tweeters). Twitter posts were projected in a cascading fashion on a screen behind the speaker.

2   Learners use an augmented reality application on their mobile devices that reacts to a user's location in the display area of an art gallery. Students' augmented view consists of virtual information on their device screens, superimposed over the "real" object they are focused on.

3   Recording device was used for lecture casting to an existing institutional learning management system. Students download resources, including podcasts, to low-cost playback devices (mobile devices). Queries that arose from listening to podcasts were sent as a message to an anonymous Q & A tool within the learning management system.

Against the background of the iPAC framework, well-designed digital learning settings are characterized as internal and individualized (personalization),

Table 4.1 Example scoring with iPAC framework

	Use Twitter at conference	*Augmented learning in art gallery*	*Podcasts of lectures*
PERSONALIZATION			
Agency	weak	weak	weak
Customization	medium	medium	weak
AUTHENTICITY			
Task	strong	medium	weak
Tool	strong	medium	weak
Setting	strong	medium	weak
COLLABORATION			
Conversation	strong	weak	weak
Data sharing	strong	weak	medium

Table 4.2 iPAC framework and possible effect sizes

realistic and practitioner-liked (authenticity), as well as networked and productive (collaboration). And it shows: Digitalization is not an automatic process. Poorly designed digital learning settings are possible as well and are characterized as external and unified (personalization), decontextualized, artifical, and contrived (authenticity), as well as solitary and consuming (collaboration). The decisive aspect is therefore, again, the expertise of teachers.

Against this background, the idea of an evidence-based approach and the idea of evaluating instruction processes with the help of effect sizes can be introduced. Although these ideas can only be implemented in the context of the iPAC framework to a limited extent, their integration is worthwhile (see Table 4.2).

Caution is required regarding seeing high scores in the iPAC framework as a guarantee of learning success. They may indicate that the instructional design of the digital learning setting has taken place at a high level. However, this does not guarantee learning success. It should also be noted that traditional media can achieve high scores in the iPAC framework, too. Learning 4.0 is therefore not reserved for digital media.

Combining the SAMR model and the iPAC framework: An integrative model

Before trying to combine the SAMR model and the iPAC framework, it seems helpful to record the advantages on both sides.

Advantages of the SAMR model are:

- At first glance, the SAMR model with its four levels appears much clearer than the iPAC framework model with its three main categories and seven subcategories.
- In the SAMR model, the layers are more abstract, but can be concretized by means of examples. The explanation of each level with the same work assignment for the learners quickly makes the meaning of the individual levels tangible.
- The SAMR model clearly highlights the benefits of digital media at the top two levels. Thus the SAMR model is an important tool, especially with regard to the formulation of tasks.
- The SAMR model helps to clearly distinguish work with digital media from work with traditional media.

Advantages of the iPAC framework are:

- A closer look at the subcategories reveals that these are like a checklist for the teacher, which he or she can use for the planning, implementation, and evaluation of learning processes with digital media.
- The iPAC framework has a clear structure due to its binary division.
- Concrete suggestions for programs or teaching ideas are particularly important for teachers who have so far used digital media in class like traditional media.

If you compare the SAMR model with the iPAC framework against this background, the individual, differentiated, cooperative, and production-oriented work on realistic tasks can be found in both models. In the iPAC framework, the points mentioned under authenticity and personalization are instructional principles that should also be observed when using traditional media, but cooperation or rather data sharing is something that can only be achieved with digital media. The SAMR model also emphasizes communication and collaboration across time and spatial boundaries. These elements are therefore decisive for the benefits of digital media in both models. They mark a learning 4.0 as explained above. This is characterized by a high degree of cognitive and social networking.

The difference between the two working models is the ranking in the SAMR model compared to the binary structure in the iPAC framework. It should be emphasized and it is worthwhile to mention that the ends of the binary structure of the sub-constructs cannot be weighed against each other. While the SAMR model focuses on the possible effects in comparison with traditional media, the iPAC framework only lists weak and strong characteristics when using digital media. The question of effect sizes and evidence is not explicitly discussed in the iPAC framework, but it can easily be integrated.

The abstraction level of the models is also different. While the SAMR model is more of a general guideline, supported by examples, the iPAC framework has concrete points on which the teacher can orientate him- or herself.

All in all, the SAMR model and the iPAC framework have different foundations, but nevertheless pursue a common goal: Learning 4.0. Both help to answer the question: How do poorly designed digital learning settings differ from well-designed digital learning settings?

The combinatorics in Table 4.3—a sort of integrative and evidence-based working model for designing digital learning settings—are intended to illustrate what has been said.

Table 4.3 Integration of SAMR model and iPAC framework

			SAMR			
			Substitution	Augmentation	Modification	Redefinition
iPAC		Personalization (Agency & Customization)	weak	weak to middle	middle to strong	strong
		Autenthicity (Task, Tool, & Setting)	weak	weak to middle	middle to strong	strong
		Collaboration (Conversation & Data sharing)	weak	weak to middle	middle to strong	strong

The use of digital media at the level of substitution therefore generates digital learning settings that are rather external and unified (personalization), decontexualized, artifical, and contrived (authenticity), as well as solitary and consumptive (collaboration), and thus have low scores in the principal constructs of the iPAC framework, "personalization," "authenticity," and "collaboration," and their seven sub-constructs. In contrast, the use of digital media at the level of redefinition leads to digital learning settings that are rather internal and individualized (personalization), realistic and practitioner-like (authenticity), as well as networked and productive (collaboration), and thus have high scores in the principal constructs of the iPAC framework, "personalization," "authenticity," and "collaboration," and their seven sub-constructs.

If these thoughts are brought together and transferred to learning 4.0, as presented above, it becomes visible: Both the SAMR model and the iPAC framework focus on learning that leads to strong social and cognitive connectivity. The upper levels of the SAMR model make this clear as the possible higher scores of the seven sub-constructs in the iPAC framework. Learning 4.0 therefore takes place in this area.

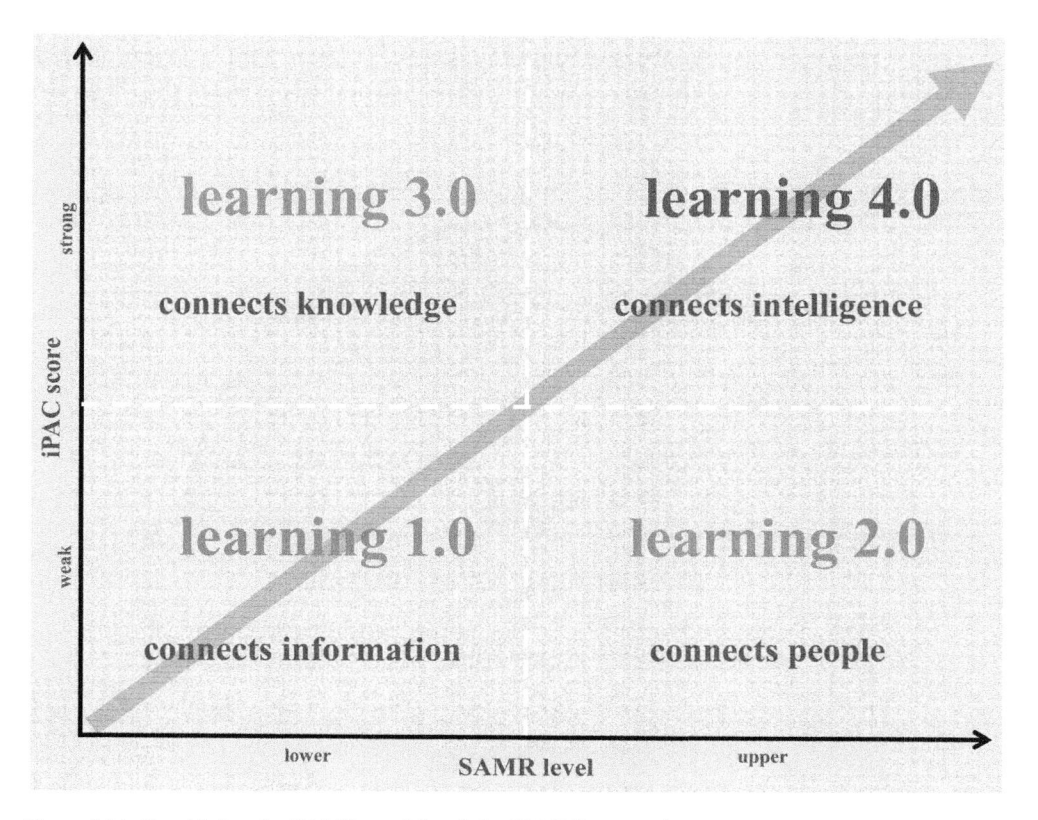

Figure 4.11 Combining the SAMR model and the iPAC framework

It has already been pointed out several times that this learning 4.0, marked by a high degree of social and cognitive connectivity, is not excluded from digital media. Rather, learning settings with traditional media are also able to do this. But, and this should be a decisive aspect in view of the numerous discussions on the benefits of digitalization, only digital media are able to enable social and cognitive connectivity nearly independent of time and space.

Conclusion: The question of why

The ideas presented above point to an aspect that determines the possibilities and limits of digitalization in education: What goals do we want to achieve with digital learning? This question does not just place the why next to the how but thrusts it into the center of attention. This is important, because it is something that is all too often lost sight of in educational policy debates: One argues over the what and the how without having first settled the question of why.

What does empirical educational research tell us about the target dimensions of instruction, and what consequences does this suggest for digitalization in education? It is again helpful to take a look at Visible Learning (cf., on the following, Hattie & Zierer, 2017).

The factor "goals" achieves an effect size of 0.68 in Visible Learning. It is closely related to a number of other factors, particularly the factor "Piagetian

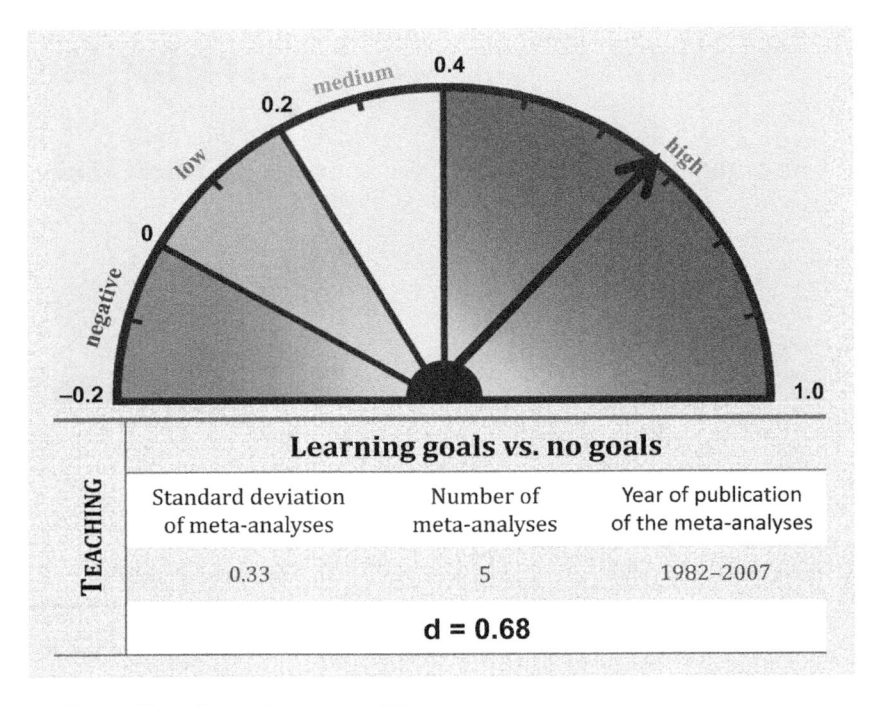

Figure 4.12 Factor "Learning goals vs. no goals"

programs," which has an effect size of 1.28 and thus calls attention to the fact that learning processes are more successful to the degree that teachers take into account their students' prior knowledge and experiences and take them as the basis for their instruction. This implies that it is necessary to define goals at different levels, an issue I will discuss in more detail below. Another important point in this context is that these are not the goals one finds specified in curricula. Curricular goals are much too distant from the learners and the concrete instructional situation to meet all the criteria good goals need to meet. An author who has written a lot about good instructional goals is Robert F. Mager. He defines the following three criteria (cf. Hattie & Zierer, 2017):

1   They need to describe observable behaviors that the learners should exhibit by the end of the lesson (e.g., writing down, calculating, reading off).

2   They need to name conditions for monitoring the learners' behavior (e.g., how much time is allowed to complete the assignment, which aids are permitted, whether they may work together with other learners).

3   They need to specify standards of evaluation for determining whether and to what extent the learners have achieved the goal (e.g., how many of the tasks need to be completed correctly).

This also illustrates why the advice "Do your best!" heard so often in pedagogical contexts is not very helpful for the learning process. It is much too vague, too imprecise, and too arbitrary to allow a detailed and compelling analysis. If, for example, a runner sets the goal of doing his best on a 10-kilometer course, how is he supposed to assess his run? He is better off setting a concrete time as a goal and attempting to achieve it—such as running the 10 kilometers in less than 60 minutes. Hence, we see that this factor also demonstrates that students need a challenge in order to learn. In addition, it alludes to one of the key points of successful goals: It is not enough for teachers to be clear about the goals of their instruction. As important as this is, it is only the first step. The second step involves seeing to it that this clarity is also present in the learners by reaching an understanding with them as to how the learning should proceed and making the criteria for successful learning visible.

The most important thing about both of these steps is the task already touched upon above of defining goals at different levels, because ultimately it is appropriate goals that will provide clarity for the teacher and a transparent learning process for the learners. A look into the literature reveals that there are several different suggestions and methods for defining learning goals at different levels. The most well known internationally are the SOLO model ("structure of observed learning outcomes") by John Biggs and Kevin Collins (1992) and the DOK model ("depth of knowledge") by Norman L. Webb (1997). Common models in the German-speaking world include the learning taxonomy developed by the German Council of Education (1970) and the various levels of challenge, usually I–VI, defined in the competence orientation approach (cf. Prenzel et al., 2014). They all go back to the taxonomy of learning goals developed by Benjamin Bloom (1984), one of the first attempts at constructing such a model. A comparison of these approaches (Table 4.4) shows that the similarities between them are greater than the differences.

One striking similarity is that these models all make a distinction between surface and deep understanding. It should be noted that one level is not better than the other from a pedagogical standpoint. Rather, one builds on the other and therefore serves as the basis for it. Moreover, there is general agreement in the literature on the point that it is always better to have a taxonomy of learning goals in mind when planning instruction.

The significance of goals and learning taxonomies suggests the idea of connecting them to the SAMR model. It should therefore come as no surprise that possibilities are being discussed for how to connect the question of why with the question of how in the context of digitalization in education. Many of these suggestions are unfortunately guided by the erroneous assumption that there is a straightforward logical connection between the level of digitalization and level of challenge—according to the principle the higher the level of digitalization, the higher the level of challenge. This idea also crops up in work influenced by Ruben C. Puentedura. A particularly graphic example is the Pedagogy Wheel.

The Pedagogy Wheel refers both to the levels of digitalization "substitution," "augmentation," "modification," and "redefinition," and to Bloom's taxonomy. Moreover, it lists several programs that can be particularly helpful in combining these two approaches. The Pedagogy Wheel thus works under the aforementioned assumption that a higher level of digitalization results in a higher level of challenge and that one can generate surface or deep understanding depending on the app one is using. Accordingly, certain digital solutions aim per se at a higher level of challenge, whereas others focus per se only on lower levels of challenge.

However, the combination of these two models is not correct from a didactic standpoint. While it might seem fitting in an idealized sense, it is not realistic

Table 4.4 Methods for defining learning goals

	SOLO Model	DOK Model	Learning taxonomy by the German Council of Education	Taxonomy by Bloom	Competence orientation approach
Surface understanding	Unistructural	Recall & Reproduction	Reproduction	Remember	Level I
				Understand	Level II
	Multistructural	Skills & Concepts	Reorganization	Apply	Level III
Deep understanding	Relational	Strategic Thinking & Reasoning	Transfer	Analyze	Level IV
				Evaluate	Level V
	Extended Abstract	Extended Thinking	Problem solving	Create	Level VI

and is therefore of little help for instructional practice. The following three explanations serve to back up this claim.

First of all, no medium leads per se to learning. The question of whether learning occurs depends primarily on whether the teacher took into account the initial learning level of the students to the extent that they are capable of deriving new knowledge using the media they were provided with. A digital method that allows for a high degree of cognitive and social connectivity and that is thus capable of supporting thinking at the highest level of challenge, for instance, can fail to achieve an effect if it is integrated into the learning process too early. The effect size of 0.26 and standard deviation of the meta-analyses of 0.33 achieved by the factor "problem-based learning" serves to illustrate this point (cf. Hattie & Zierer, 2017). A digital learning method like that described above will be too demanding for learners located at the level of surface understanding and possibly even produce negative effects, but it can lead to far-reaching and lasting learning gains in those capable of learning at the level of deep understanding.

Second, no medium leads per se to learning at a certain level of challenge. Even if learning processes have been initiated and the media are appropriate for bringing about knowledge gains, the question of whether learning occurs at the level of surface understanding or at the level of deep understanding is not answered by the medium. In the best case it will enable learning—and in the worst case it will hinder learning. The most important thing is rather to set a goal

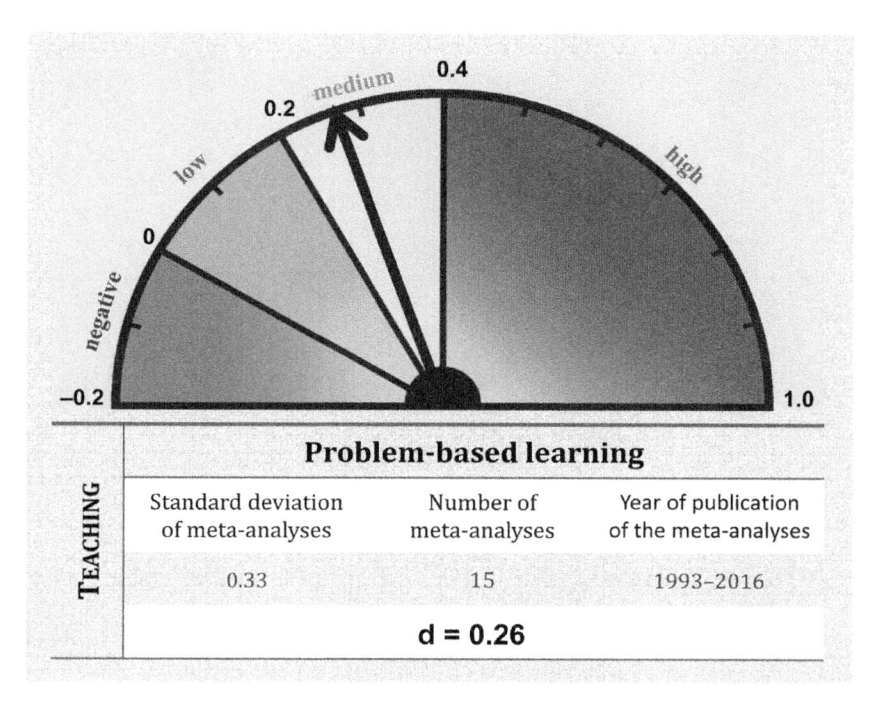

Figure 4.13 Factor "Problem-based learning"

in the learning process and to implement it by making decisions on the content, the method, and the media. For example, the digital method outlined above can also fail to achieve an effect in learners who have already reached the level of deep understanding if the teacher asks them to learn in the same way repeatedly without formulating a new goal, because then the learning in question will consist of nothing more than a form of reproduction and reorganization. This line of thought demonstrates that the widely held belief that digitalization in education will revolutionize learning per se is incorrect.

Third, digital methods are not the only methods that lead to learning at a higher level of challenge. The belief just alluded to suggests that only digitalization has the power to produce a high level of cognitive and social connectivity. As already demonstrated above, this is not necessarily the case. On the contrary, it is clear that traditional media can also have this power. A piece of paper and a pencil is often all it takes to bring people together with their thoughts, ideas, and visions. A simple glance at the factor "cooperative learning," which achieves an effect size of 0.40, should be enough to substantiate this claim with empirical evidence. Cooperative learning methods aligned toward the think-pair-share strategy, such as group puzzle, fishbowl, and placemat activities, can produce a high degree of cognitive and social connectivity when implemented in a traditional analogue form—if the teacher has reflected on and defined the goals in advance.

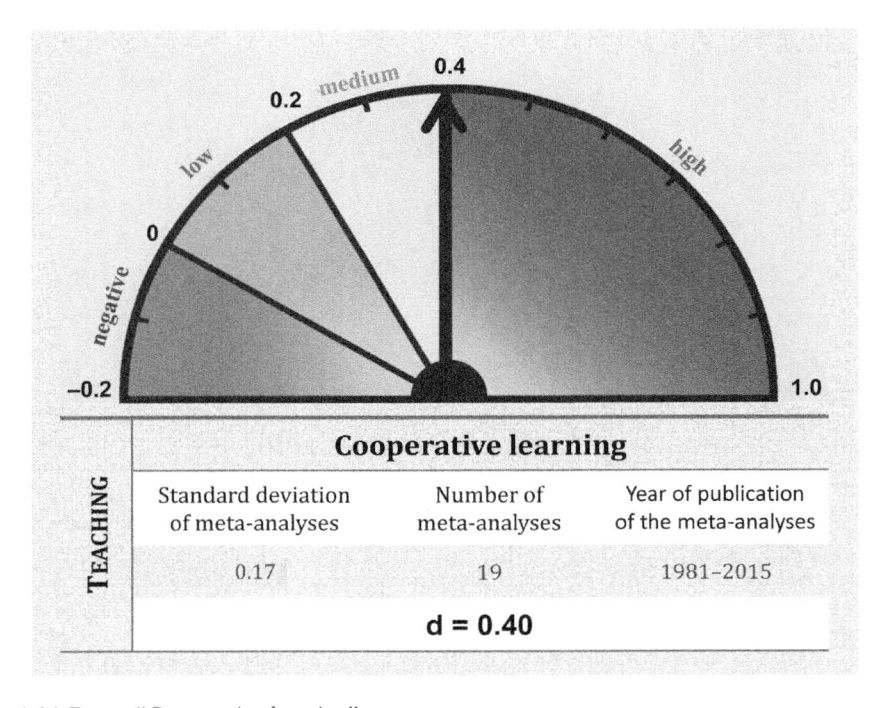

Figure 4.14 Factor "Cooperative learning"

Hence, the important factor in combining the SAMR model with the various levels of challenge is to consider the question of "why" before the question of "how." Wolfgang Klafki (1996) already formulated this idea in his critical-constructive didactics with the principle of giving didactics primacy over methodology. In other words, the goals must be clearly defined before it is possible to engage in any meaningful reflection on methods.

This conclusion recalls debates on instructional methods—which have been particularly passionate in the German-speaking world: Is open instruction or closed instruction better? Although this terminology is overly simplistic and such a dualism reductionistic in view of the wide range of instructional possibilities, it does get at the core of the problem. The place of school education is not the method. The place of school education is the interaction between human beings.

Methods can support, optimize, and foster this reaction, but they cannot replace it. The key question with regard to instructional methods is thus whether they help to enable interaction between people, to influence learning and teaching in a positive sense, and ultimately to achieve the instructional goal. If the methods the teacher applies do not serve these purposes, then they were the wrong methods to choose from a didactic standpoint.

The same thing applies to digitalization in education. The question of whether digital learning or non-digital learning is better is beside the point. Digitalization is not and should not be made into an end in itself. Its purpose should rather consist in facilitating interactions between people and exerting a positive influence on teaching and learning processes. Wherever the digital replaces the social, where the digital takes away the challenge of learning, where the digital separates people instead of bringing them together, where typing takes the place of speaking, it has failed to achieve its purpose.

The matrix in Table 4.5 can help you reflect on the issues raised in this chapter. It is intended as a generalization for orientation purposes and as a general didactic working model. As such, it provides support in planning concrete lessons and includes two steps for reflection that need to be completed in sequence before they can be combined.

Table 4.5 Matrix for self-reflection

		2. Reflection process			
1. Reflection process		*S* **iPAC**	*A* **iPAC**	*M* **iPAC**	*R* **iPAC**
	Surface understanding				
	Deep understanding				

The first step in the reflection process involves deciding what goals to pursue, that is, why one wishes to initiate learning processes and what purpose they are to serve. The second step then consists of deciding which media are helpful and which are not at the various levels of digitalization. It goes without saying, and is also a basic general didactic principle, that the second step should not be viewed separately from the first step but that the two should be seen as interdependent. However, the question of goals is still more important for the educational process than the question of media. It is therefore advisable to reflect once again on whether the goals are appropriate after one has selected the media. In this way, the question of "why" forms both the starting point and the goal of didactic thinking and action.

Based on the iPAC Framework survey (cf. www.mobilelearningtoolkit.com/ipac-surveys.html), the questionnaire in Table 4.6 was developed. It contains a block of questions about the SAMR model as well as the iPAC framework and can be helpful from the teacher's point of view to question the choice and integration of digital media in the learning setting. Apart from the block of questions about the SAMR model, it can also be answered by learners and thus, in addition to self-assessment, provide an important external assessment.

Table 4.6 Questionnaire for evaluating the use of digital media

	I strongly disagree				I strongly agree
	1	2	3	4	5
SAMR level					
Digital media are used to substitute traditional media.	O	O	O	O	O
Digital media are used to augment traditional media.	O	O	O	O	O
Digital media are used to modify traditional media.	O	O	O	O	O
Digital media are used to redefine traditional media.	O	O	O	O	O
iPAC–Personalization					
Students choose the place(s) to work (classroom, home, playground etc.).	O	O	O	O	O
Students decide the time to work (during class, after school, at weekends etc.).	O	O	O	O	O
Students decide what they want to learn (choosing their own question, task, problem, and project etc.).	O	O	O	O	O
Students chose how to work (using textbooks, online material etc.).	O	O	O	O	O
Students customize the settings on their device.	O	O	O	O	O
iPAC–Authenticity					
Students learn in a place suggested by the topic.	O	O	O	O	O
Students learn in a realistic or virtual space.	O	O	O	O	O
Students work in a similar way to an expert (collecting data, sharing findings, composing material etc.).	O	O	O	O	O
Students participate in a genuine, real-world community activity.	O	O	O	O	O
Students make their learning relevant to their lives.	O	O	O	O	O

	I strongly disagree				I strongly agree
	1	2	3	4	5
Students consider experts' views on the topic (via Twitter, Skype etc.).	O	O	O	O	O
iPAC-Collaboration					
Learners participate in peer face-to-face discussions about the work.	O	O	O	O	O
Learners participate in peer online discussions about the work.	O	O	O	O	O
Learners discuss the work online with people they **don't** know (scientist, artist etc.).	O	O	O	O	O
Learners work together and create a digital product (video, podcast, photo etc.).	O	O	O	O	O
Learners exchange digital content with others online.	O	O	O	O	O
Learners share and compare digital content generated on their device with others.	O	O	O	O	O

According to the considerations made, the score of the SAMR model questions can be linked to the score of the iPAC framework questions. The higher the SAMR level, the higher the score in the iPAC framework. If there are differences, it is advisable to reconsider the planning. In the same way, it will be necessary to critically examine the learning arrangement if learners arrive at different assessments after instruction than you do.

Summary

WHAT WAS RUBEN C. PUENTEDURA'S INTENTION IN DEVELOPING THE SAMR MODEL?

Ruben C. Puentedura developed the SAMR model as an aid to orientation and therefore as a general didactic working model for making learning 4.0 visible. SAMR is an acronym for the four levels of digitalization he identified: substitution, augmentation, modification, and redefinition.

WHAT CHARACTERIZES DIGITALIZATION AT THE LEVELS OF SUBSTITUTION, AUGMENTATION, MODIFICATION, AND REDEFINITION?

The levels of digitalzation describe how new media can be applied in comparision to traditional media. In connection with this, they provide an idealized illustration of how progressing to a higher level enables a higher degree of social and cognitive connectivity between learners.

WHAT WAS THE INTENTION IN DEVELOPING THE IPAC FRAMEWORK?

A group of researchers and teacher educators developed the iPAC framework to distinguish well-designed digital learning settings from poorly designed digital learning settings. At the center of the iPAC framework is the notion that digital learning has the potential to transcend the spatial and temporal restrictions of traditional education and learning.

WHAT CHARACTERIZES DIGITALIZATION FROM THE POINT OF VIEW OF THE THREE PRINCIPAL CONSTRUCTS "PERSONALIZATION," "AUTHENTICITY," AND "COLLABORATION"?

Personalization, authenticity, and collaboration present the three principal constructs of the iPAC framework. They were distinguished into seven sub-constructs: Personalization includes agency and customization; authenticity includes task, tools, and setting; and collaboration includes conversation and production.

HOW CAN THE SAMR MODEL AND THE IPAC FRAMEWORK BE COMBINED?

The SAMR model and the iPAC framework are to be located on different levels, but still pursue a common goal. Therefore, they can be combined with each other. The result is a planning and evaluation matrix which can be helpful in distingushing well-designed digital learning settings from poorlu designed ones.

WHY IS "WHY" THE MOST IMPORTANT QUESTION TO ASK WITH REGARD TO THE USE OF MEDIA?

No medium leads per se to learning, let alone to learning at a high level of challenge. In order for learning to occur, the medium must be integrated into the learning process in an appropriate and meaningful way. The key criterion for this is the question of "why." It is therefore important from a didactic standpoint to set and reflect on the goals of a lesson before answering the question of "how." For the latter, the SAMR model combined with the iPAC framework delivers substantial information.

5

Teacher professionalism is key

Task for reflection

Reflect on how the ideas discussed in this book have changed your competencies as well as your mindframes concerning digitalization in education: What was new to you? What do you consider particularly important? What would you like to keep working on?

Goals

This chapter brings the argumentation down to the most important point: Teachers matter the most. When you finish reading this chapter, you should be able to answer the following questions:

- What makes up teacher professionalization, and what consequences does it have for digitalization in education?
- Why is the factor "outdoor/adventure programs" so effective, and what conclusions does this suggest for learning 4.0?
- Why is focusing on human beings the most important factor of successful digital learning?

There is no doubt that structures are also important in times of digitalization. Digital learning cannot be realized without functioning equipment. But structures do not have an intrinsic effect. Digital learning needs human beings to breathe life into it.

There are a couple of well-known quotations attributed to Bill Gates, the founder of Microsoft and therefore doubtlessly an advocate of new media:

> Teachers need to teach differently in the age of the infobahn. That's true, but they are still needed. The children don't just want to sit at home in

front of a screen and suck in the material they're supposed to learn. They need the group, they need the human aspect, they need teachers.

And: "Technology is just a tool in terms of getting the kids working together and motivating them, the teacher is the most important."

It might come as a surprise for some to hear a person from this sector of the economy make a statement like this. Yet perhaps it is not so surprising after all: Who is better qualified to say what makes up successful digitalization than a person who deals with the possibilities and limits of digitalization on a daily basis?

In essence, then, it is clearly about human beings. All the technology developed in the course of digitalization always needs people to make it effective. And what do people need to achieve these effects with the help of digitalization? This is the issue I will focus on in the following.

What is teacher expertise?

If we leave the ideological extremes out of the discussion and take a realistic look at what is known today about the use of computers, tablets, interactive whiteboards, and other similar innovations, we must come to the conclusion that technology will not revolutionize learning all on its own. No "new" medium in the history of school has achieved this: not the pencil, not the blackboard, not the textbook, not the computer, not the tablet, and not the interactive whiteboard either. Technology always needs people to be effective. Hence, the place of education in teaching and learning processes is not the medium. Rather, the place of education in teaching and learning processes should be seen as lying in the interaction between human beings. The important thing is hence what teachers do with the technology—in which situations they turn it on and in which situations they turn it off.

And yet it is one of the most persistent myths in the educational discussion that a successful teacher is one who possesses a particularly high degree of subject matter competence. Our entire teacher education system is grounded on this assumption. It accordingly receives the most attention in teacher education curricula, and whenever there is a discussion of reform, it is always accompanied by a call for more subject matter competence. This remains true in times of digitalization: We need teachers who are experts in working with new media. As important as this expertise is, however, it will not be enough. In fact, it will not even be the decisive factor on its own. This may be illustrated with the help of the factor "teacher subject matter knowledge":

How can it be that teacher subject matter knowledge achieves a hardly measureable effect of 0.11 on student learning performance in Visible Learning (cf. Hattie, 2013; for a discussion, cf. Zierer, 2014), whereas the few German-language studies on this issue appear to arrive at other conclusions (cf. Baumert & Kunter, 2006; Blömeke, Kaiser, & Lehmann, 2010; Kunter et al., 2011; Pant

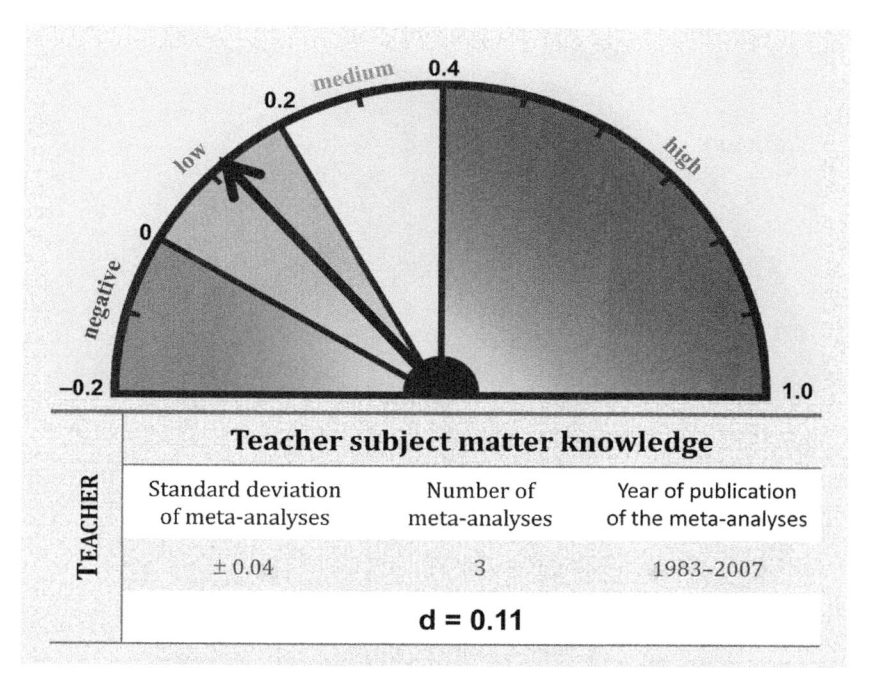

Figure 5.1 Factor "Teacher subject matter knowledge"

et al., 2013)? If we understand instruction as an interaction between students and the teacher on the subject matter, an explanation is easy to find (cf. Zierer, 2015b): We all know people who know a whole lot but are unable to explain it. They lack didactic competence. And we also know people who know a whole lot but are so unapproachable that it is impossible to build up a relationship with them. These people lack pedagogical competence. Hence, subject matter competence alone is not a sufficient condition for successful instruction. It needs to be accompanied by didactic and pedagogical competence—and only with them can it achieve the desired effect. While this does not mean that subject matter knowledge is unnecessary, the answer does not lie in demanding even more competence. What we really need is not more subject matter knowledge but instruction that brings the great store of knowledge we already have to life. And that requires didactic and pedagogical competence. Figure 5.2 provides a summary of these considerations (cf. Zierer, 2015b, and Hattie & Zierer, 2017):

This reasoning is borne out by the German-language studies mentioned above, at least when one reads them in the right way. What the IQB state comparision (cf. Pant et al., 2013) investigates, for instance, is whether teachers who have studied a subject give more successful instruction than those who have not studied that particular subject. And the results show that this is indeed the case. Yet taking this to mean that more subject matter competence automatically leads to better instruction falls short of the mark, because the teachers who studied a

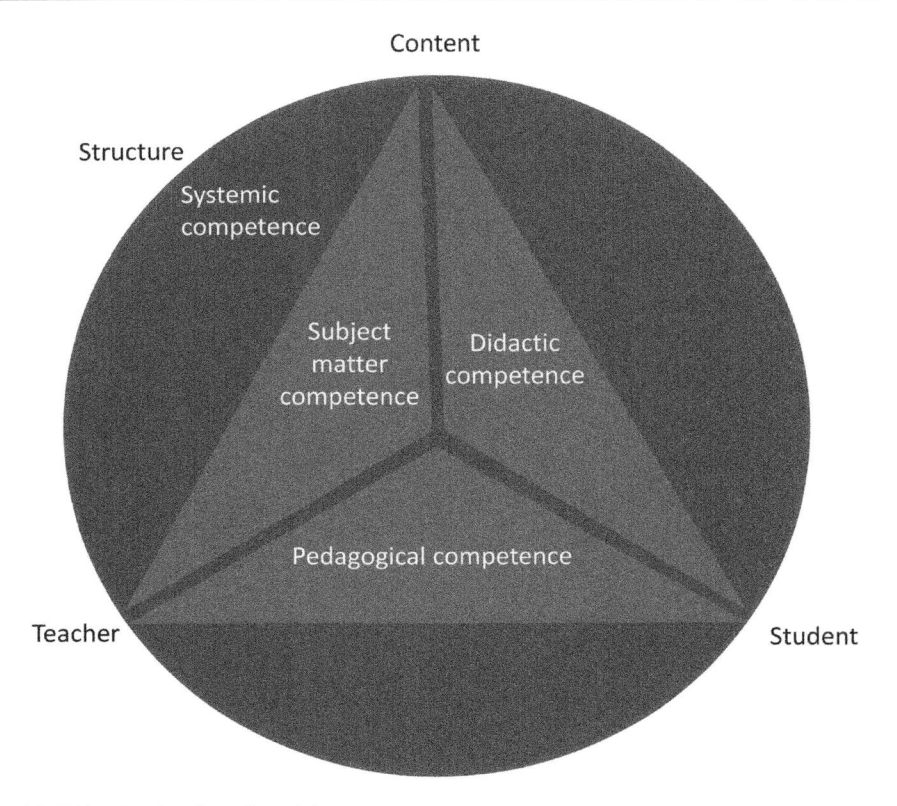

Figure 5.2 Didactic triangle and teaching competences

particular subject managed to improve their didactic and pedagogical competence primarily during the practical training phase of their education.

The considerations made can be linked to the Technological Pedagogical Content Knowledge (TPACK) framework. This is one of the best-known and most discussed models of teacher professionalization in the context of digitalization. For this reason, it is explained by quoting Matthew J. Koehler and Punya Mishra, two of the creators of the TPACK framework in more detail (cf. Koehler & Mishra, 2009; Mishra & Koehler, 2006):

Technological Pedagogical Content Knowledge (TPACK attempts to identify the nature of knowledge required by teachers for technology integration in their teaching, while addressing the complex, multifaceted and situated nature of teacher knowledge. The TPACK framework extends Shulman's idea of Pedagogical Content Knowledge (Figure 5.3).

The complex interplay of three primary forms of knowledge is at the heart of the TPACK framework, consisting of: Content Knowledge (CK), Pedagogy Knowledge (PK), and Technology Knowledge (TK). The TPACK framework goes beyond seeing these three knowledge bases in isolation. It goes further by emphasizing the kinds of knowledge that lie at the intersections between three

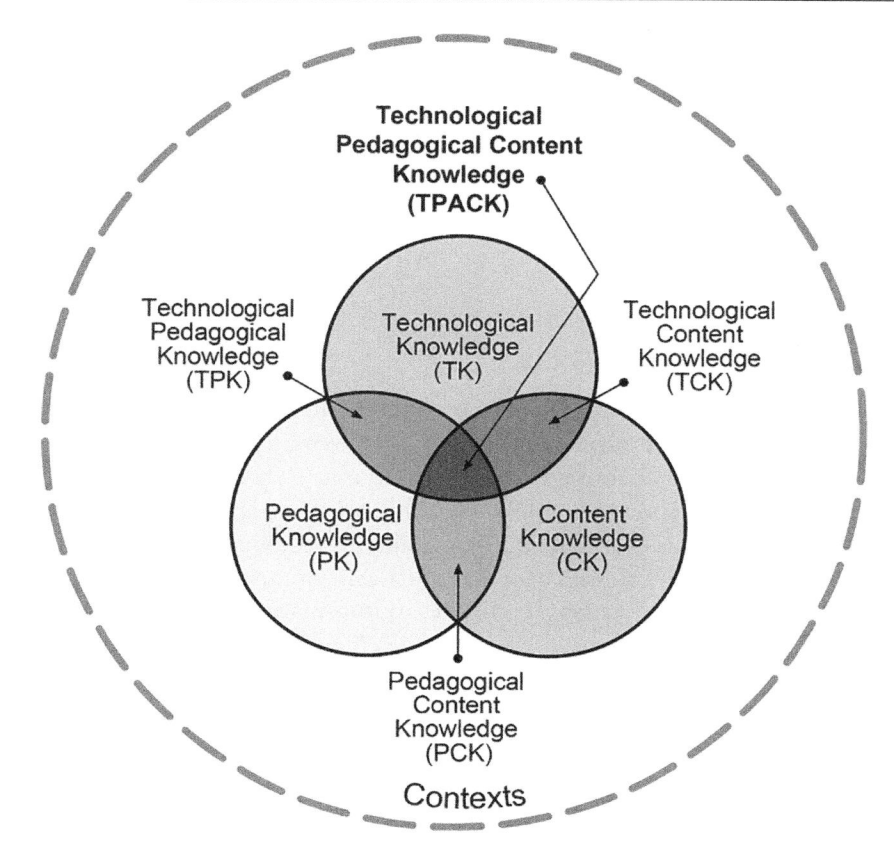

Figure 5.3 TPACK

Reproduced by permission of the publisher, © tpack.org, 2012

primary forms: Pedagogical Content Knowledge (PCK), Technological Content Knowledge (TCK), Technological Pedagogical Knowledge (TPK), and Technological Pedagogical Content Knowledge (TPACK). All of these will now be explained in more detail.

Content Knowledge (CK):

Teachers' knowledge about the subject matter to be learned or taught. The content to be covered in middle school science or history is different from the content to be covered in an undergraduate course on art appreciation or a graduate seminar on astrophysics . . . As Shulman (1986) noted, this knowledge would include knowledge of concepts, theories, ideas, organizational frameworks, knowledge of evidence and proof, as well as established practices and approaches toward developing such knowledge.

(Koehler & Mishra, 2009, p. 63)

Pedagogical Knowledge (PK):

Teachers' deep knowledge about the processes and practices or methods of teaching and learning. They encompass, among other things, overall educational purposes, values, and aims. This generic form of knowledge applies to understanding how students learn, general classroom management skills, lesson planning, and student assessment.

(Koehler & Mishra, 2009, p. 64)

Technology Knowledge (TK):

Knowledge about certain ways of thinking about, and working with technology, tools and resources, and working with technology can apply to all technology tools and resources. This includes understanding information technology broadly enough to apply it productively at work and in everyday life, being able to recognize when information technology can assist or impede the achievement of a goal, and being able continually adapt to changes in information technology.

(Koehler & Mishra, 2009, p. 65)

Pedagogical Content Knowledge (PCK):

Consistent with and similar to Shulman's idea of knowledge of pedagogy that is applicable to the teaching of specific content. Central to Shulman's conceptualization of PCK is the notion of the transformation of the subject matter for teaching. Specifically, according to Shulman (1986), this transformation occurs as the teacher interprets the subject matter, finds multiple ways to represent it, and adapts and tailors the instructional materials to alternative conceptions and students' prior knowledge. PCK covers the core business of teaching, learning, curriculum, assessment and reporting, such as the conditions that promote learning and the links among curriculum, assessment, and pedagogy.

(Koehler & Mishra, 2009, p. 65)

Technological Content Knowledge (TCK):

An understanding of the manner in which technology and content influence and constrain one another. Teachers need to master more than the subject matter they teach; they must also have a deep understanding of the manner in which the subject matter (or the kinds of representations that can be constructed) can be changed by the application of particular technologies. Teachers need to understand which specific technologies are best suited for addressing subject-matter learning in their domains and how the content dictates or perhaps even changes the technology—or vice versa.

(Koehler & Mishra, 2009, p. 65)

Technological Pedagogical Knowledge (TPK):

An understanding of how teaching and learning can change when particular technologies are used in particular ways. This includes knowing the pedagogical affordances and constraints of a range of technological tools as they relate to disciplinarily and developmentally appropriate pedagogical designs and strategies.

(Koehler & Mishra, 2009, p. 66)

Technological Pedagogical Content Knowledge (TPACK):

Underlying truly meaningful and deeply skilled teaching with technology, TPACK is different from knowledge of all three concepts individually. Instead, TPACK is the basis of effective teaching with technology, requiring an understanding of the representation of concepts using technologies; pedagogical techniques that use technologies in constructive ways to teach content; knowledge of what makes concepts difficult or easy to learn and how technology can help redress some of the problems that students face; knowledge of students' prior knowledge and theories of epistemology; and knowledge of how technologies can be used to build on existing knowledge to develop new epistemologies or strengthen old ones.

(Koehler & Mishra, 2009, p. 66)

Effective technology integration for pedagogy around specific subject matter requires developing sensitivity to the dynamic, transactional relationship between these components of knowledge situated in unique contexts. Individual teachers, grade-level, school-specific factors, demographics, culture, and other factors ensure that every situation is unique, and no single combination of content, technology, and pedagogy will apply for every teacher, every course, or every view of teaching (cf Koehler & Mishra, 2009, p. 67).

So far the thoughts of Koehler (2012) on the TPACK framework.

As convincing as this argumentation may sound, the triad of subject matter competence, didactic competence, and pedagogical competence as well as the seven aspects of the TPACK framework (technological knowledge, pedagogical knowledge, content knowledge, technological pedagogical knowledge, pedagogical content knowledge, technological content knowledge, and technological pedagogical content knowledge) are still not enough to produce successful instruction. Rather, we are well aware that our performance in pedagogical contexts depends not just on what we do but also, and especially, on how and why we do something. The key to success is therefore not just competence in the form of knowledge and ability but also our mindframes in the form of will and judgment—and the latter is what determines whether the former are brought into play. Again, I would like to illustrate this notion with the help of the didactic triangle in Figure 5.4 (cf. Zierer, 2015b, and Hattie & Zierer, 2017).

The current debate on inclusion can serve as an example of this idea. There are no doubt a lot of teachers who possess a high level of subject matter competence, didactic competence, and pedagogical competence, and who also have professional mindframes. One would think that this would provide a solid foundation for inclusive instruction. But what happens when government policymakers relegate tasks to the rank and file without providing them with the support they need to fulfill them and without showing their appreciation for what has been achieved so far? Teachers often feel like they have been left in the lurch in such situations, and people who do not feel understood end up developing dysfunctional mindframes. Teachers are thus in danger of losing the will to teach inclusively and also have judgments to account for this loss of will. In this state of affairs, they will not bring their competence to bear and their instruction will fail—not due to a lack of competence but because of dysfunctional mindframes.

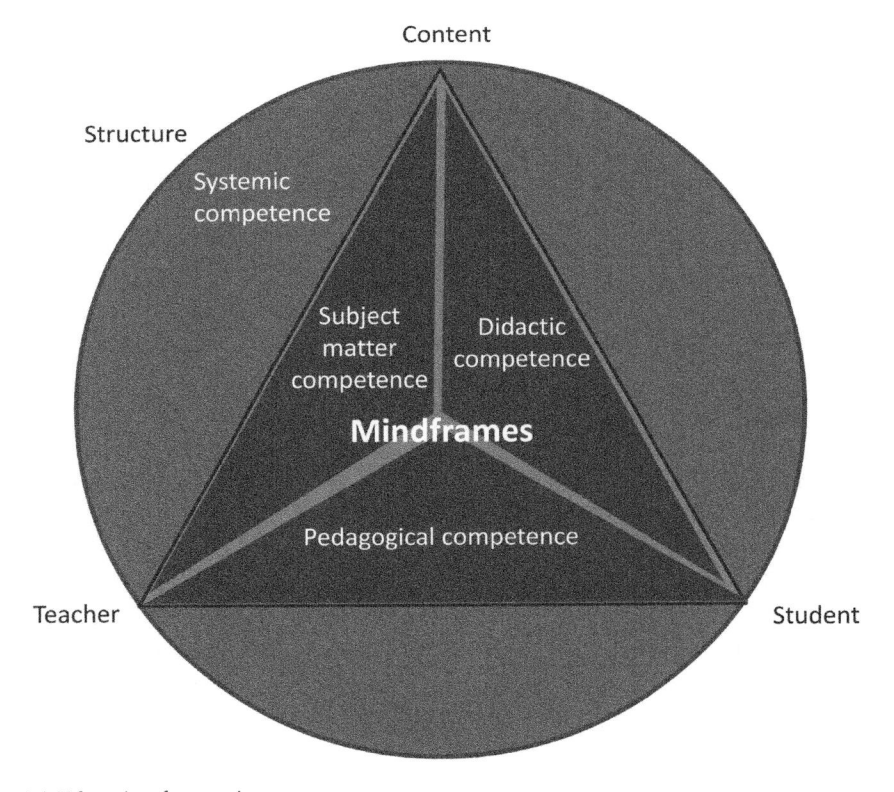

Figure 5.4 Educational expertise

To put these ideas in more concrete terms, it is worth it in this connection to take a look at findings from recent resesarch on expertise, such as the "Good Work Project" initiated by Howard Gardner, Mihaly Csíkszentmihályi, and William Damon (cf. Gardner, Csíkszentmihályi & Damon, 2005. It posits that professional success is based on three E's: excellence, engagement, and ethics. The basic idea is that only if all three aspects are present and visible will people be successful in their activities. What this means for the activity of a teacher is that successful behavior in school and instruction does not just require knowledge and ability (in this sense excellence) but also will (in this sense engagement) and judgment (in this sense ethics). Particularly interesting is the fact that there is an inner link between these aspects: Ability is based on knowledge that can only be retrieved when there is a will to do so, and since there are always reasons for doing so, this will is based on judgment. A teacher who can retrieve the necessary ability, knowledge, will, and judgment will act accordingly in a particular situation. And if the context is favorable, he or she will also be successful in this endeavor. If one of these aspects is missing, for instance the will, the teacher will in all probability fail. Figure 5.5 (ACAC model) sums up this argumentation (cf. Zierer, 2015b, and Hattie & Zierer, 2017).

Successful teachers are not just passionate about the subject they teach; they are also passionate about teaching and learning in general, about the learners, and about their profession. And this passion is not just important for becoming

Figure 5.5 ACAC model

a successful teacher. It is also important for remaining in this challenging profession and therefore for remaining a successful teacher in the long term.

If we apply these ideas to digitalization in education, we may conclude that successful digital learning is not just a question of competence but also and especially a question of mindframes.

Use the ACAC model to reflect for yourself: How do you think about digitalization? Where are your strengths, where are your weaknesses? How do ability, knowledge, will, and judgment relate to each other? The questionnaire in Table 5.1 can help you do this. Fill it out and discuss your assessments with a colleague.

At this point, an uncertainty frequently emerges over whether it is possible to change mindframes at all. Mindframes are important, but are they not something we have no influence over? As a means of answering this question, take a look back at your own life: Sometimes a single pivotal experience is enough to effect a fundamental change in our own mindframes, yet at other times we cannot seem to change them no matter how much effort we put into it. This demonstrates that developing mindframes is no easy task. Whereas competencies can be communicated in a matter of five minutes, developing mindframes clearly takes more time, more courage, more patience, and more effort. But is this a reason to shrink back from the task and neglect to take this crucial step toward professionalization? Of course not: If mindframes are so important, then accepting this challenge is an essential element in the process of professionalization. In a general sense, there are two approaches to developing mindframes. The first entails a broadening of competencies. This leads to new experiences,

Table 5.1 Questionnaire for self-reflection

	I strongly disagree				I strongly agree
	1	*2*	*3*	*4*	*5*
ABILITY					
I am very good at using digital media in the classroom.	O	O	O	O	O
I am very good at supporting learning processes with digital media.	O	O	O	O	O
KNOWLEDGE					
I know perfectly well what the benefits of digital media are.	O	O	O	O	O
I know perfectly well when it pays to use digital media.	O	O	O	O	O
WILL					
My goal is always to make the use of digital media in my lessons dependent on pedagogical considerations.	O	O	O	O	O
My goal is always to question the use of digital media in my teaching.	O	O	O	O	O
JUDGMENT					
I am thoroughly convinced that digital media are important for my teaching.	O	O	O	O	O
I am thoroughly convinced that supporting my students' learning processes through digital media is important.	O	O	O	O	O

which in turn have a lasting impact on mindframes. The second involves making explicit and critically examining existing mindframes. A combination of the two approaches works best.

But which mindframes are relevant? Which ones are called for in the task of enhancing the effectiveness of digitalization in particular and pedagogical interactions in general? The factor "outdoor/advneture programs" offers an initial approach, as it is focused like no other on the most important aspect of the educational process: the human being.

The factor "outdoor/adventure programs"

No other factor provides such a powerful illustration of what makes up successful teaching and learning processes. It is primarily teachers who also do a lot of other things right who apply such measures, whereas teachers who have a lot of room for improvement tend to avoid them, and this fact alone should make us sit up and take notice. What, then, is the secret of outdoor and adventure activities?

Programs subsumed under this factor include school camps of several days' duration, stays at youth education centers in the country, and field trips. They achieve a large effect size of 0.43. The four meta-analyses named in *Visible Learning* only include studies from the USA and Australia, but the results may

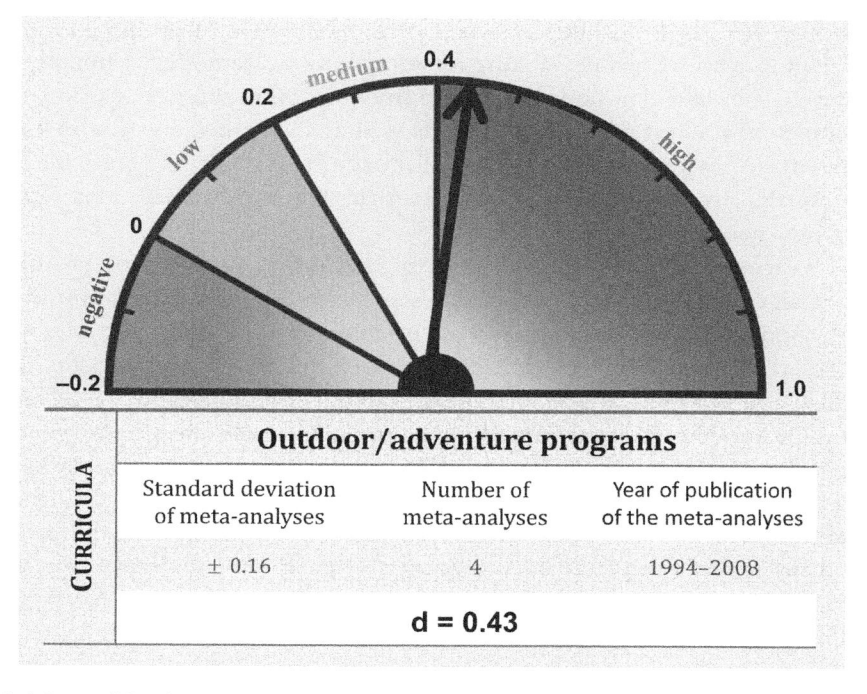

Figure 5.6 Factor "Outdoor/adventure programs"

presumably be applied to any country offering similar programs. The effects are positive across all domains tested in the studies, including mathematics, natural science, and language skills, social skills, self-concept, and motivation. Another special feature of outdoor and adventure programs is that they have follow-up effects and can therefore continue to exert influence after the the program itself ends. That is a rare outcome in the educational sciences. Much more common is a so-called washout effect, in which a measure demonstrably loses its influence after a certain time. An example of a factor in which a washout effect can be observed is "early intervention": By the end of the fourth grade, it is no longer possible to identify which children in a particular school class attended a day care center. What are the reasons for the lasting effects of outdoor and adventure programs? One reason lies in their clarity: A standout feature of successful programs in this area is that the goals, the content, the methods, and the media are clear and understandable, concrete and practicable. A second reason has to do with the fact that group activities in a stimulating environment foster teacher–student and student–student relationships. They demand cooperation and build up trust. This suggests two conclusions: First, both of these reasons may be applied to all structural, curricular, and instructional aspects. They are indispensable for successful learning. Second, it is interesting to compare this factor with structural measures, such as a lengthening of the school day. The results of a cost–benefit analysis are clear: Outdoor and adventure programs produce much greater effects than a lengthening of the school day and are also considerably less expensive.

What overall message does this allow us to derive for digitalization in education? We need teachers who see instruction not as a monologue but as a dialogue, who are always looking for something in learners that nobody knows anything about and nobody believes in anymore, who can speak passionately and competently about their knowledge as well as about their lives, who exchange information with their colleagues, collaborate with them, and treat the learners as equals, always conscious of the fact that they need the learners just as the learners need them.

Learners should be seen as the starting point for education and instruction—with all of their strengths and weaknesses. A teacher–student relationship based on cooperation and acceptance is a necessary precondition for adopting this perspective and is one of the most important factors for successful teaching and visible learning (d = 0.72). Making mistakes is nothing to be ashamed of, because mistakes provide important information along the way to giving successful instruction. This demonstrates that instruction is not a one-way street but an intensive dialogue between the learner and the teacher. Key factors for this are feedback (d = 0.75), because it is essential for communication during a lesson and about the lesson, and teacher clarity (d = 0.75), because it sets the standard for the lesson and its evaluation. Furthermore, it is undeniable that peer influences and classroom cohesion play an important part (d = 0.53)—cooperative learning, for instance, is superior to competitive learning and individualistic learning (d = 0.42). Direct instruction (d = 0.59) is a logical consequence of the line of reasoning presented here so far—not understood as frontal instruction but as a form of teaching in which the teacher uses information on the learning level of the students as a basis for determining the goals, content, methods, and media.

Focusing on human beings

In 2016 I was invited to attend the ten-year reunion of the last class of fourth-graders I had taught as an elementary school teacher in 2006. I felt very honored, so I took the long journey back to my old school upon myself and was very curious to find out how "my" students had developed in the intervening years. I learned a lot of interesting things that evening, but there was one story I found particularly remarkable: Fabian told me that he had held onto a note I had given to him and that he had taken it out to read again and again over the years. It was a source of motivation for him. I gave him an astonished look, and he showed it to me:

> "Very good, Fabian. I'm happy that you practice so much! You're on the right track!"

I stuck notes like these to the students' exercise books now and then to let them know things I considered important—a classic example of teacher-to-student

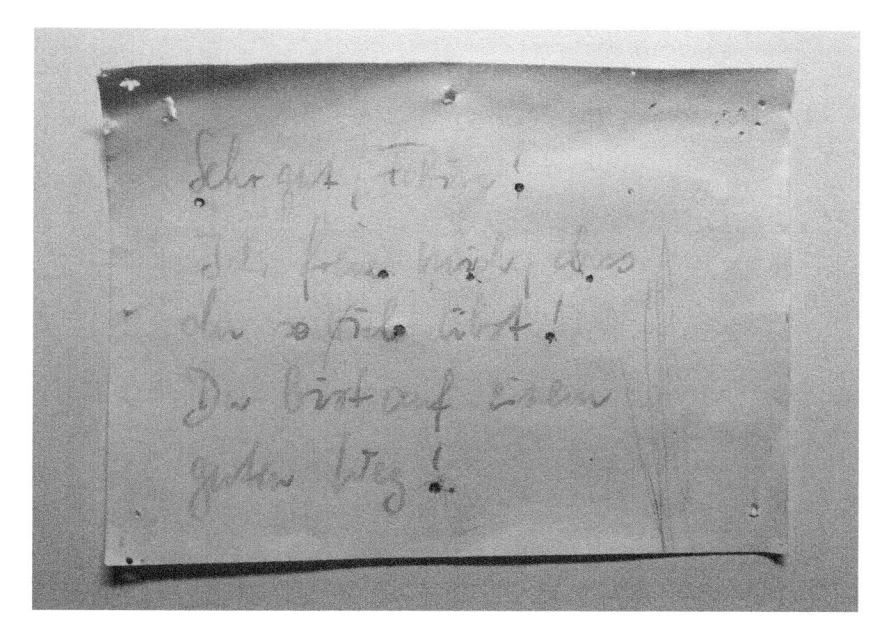

Figure 5.7 Feedback to Fabian

© Fabian Zeiher

feedback, as it were, and certainly not even the best one I could have given in this situation. The remarkable thing about this story, however, is that the medium is not the deciding factor! It might seem initially that the note itself was what had an effect on the learner. It might have conceivably also been an e-mail that he kept for years and maybe even printed out and carried around with him. However, the real reason why this piece of paper had an effect only becomes apparent upon closer consideration: The note is a symbol of the seemingly functioning relationship between human beings. For Fabian, it was and still is a sign of recognition, acceptance, esteem. For him it is the result of a pedagogical act that still has an effect ten years later. In other words, more important than what teachers do is how and why they do what they do. Hence, the place of school education is never the structure, never the method, and never the medium either. The place of school education is the interaction between human beings.

And since the success of interaction in school and instruction depends primarily on the teacher, it is only logical to focus on teacher professionalism. Professionalism reveals itself not just in teachers' competencies but also, as already explained above, in their mindframes. What it involves is essentially the willingness and the capacity to seek and to understand one's own influence. It is thus possible to define professional mindframes that inform the actions of successful teachers. The book *10 Mindframes for Visible Learning* (Hattie & Zierer, 2017) defines ten such mindframes. These mindframes determine the success of pedagogical action. Applied to the issue of digitalization, these mindframes demonstrate what digitalization in school does not mean—and also what digitalization in school can mean and how it can succeed. A few examples are given to illustrate the argumentation:

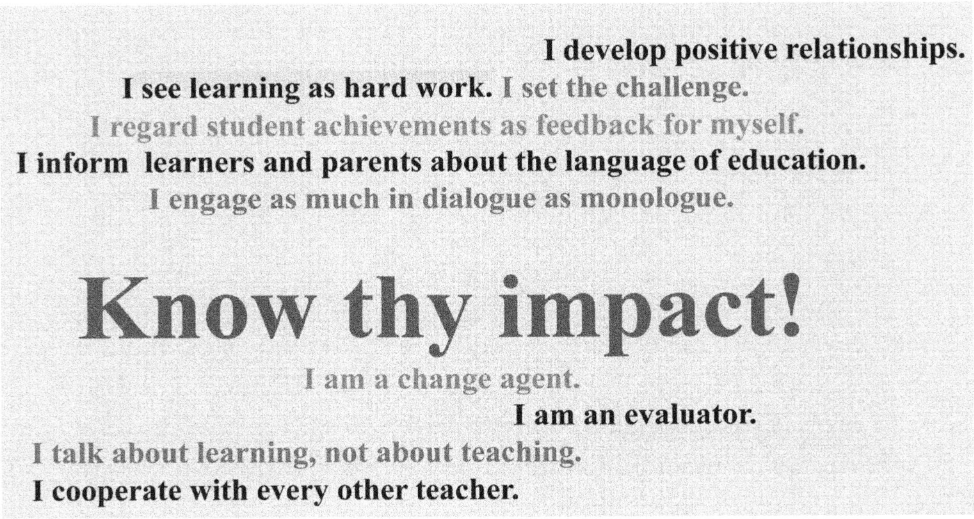

I develop positive relationships.
I see learning as hard work. I set the challenge.
I regard student achievements as feedback for myself.
I inform learners and parents about the language of education.
I engage as much in dialogue as monologue.

Know thy impact!

I am a change agent.
I am an evaluator.
I talk about learning, not about teaching.
I cooperate with every other teacher.

Figure 5.8 Know thy impact

> 1   *Successful teachers talk about learning, not about teaching. Their pedagogical and didactic considerations begin and end with the learner.* Digitalization in instruction does not mean implementing the same learning program for all of the learners. What digitalization in instruction means is rather taking into account the learners' prior knowledge and prior experiences and applying the digital methods that are most suitable for building on this knowledge and these experiences.

In recent years, a variety of digital solutions have been developed to measure the performance level of students. This data can be helpful for teachers to make their own lessons effective. There is no doubt that this measurement of the performance level can also be carried out with traditional media. But there is also no doubt that this laborious work can be done digitally as well. In this way, the teacher gains time and space to enter into a stronger exchange with students about their learning. The prerequisite for this is that the teacher is supported by the mindframe of talking about learning and not about teaching. Otherwise, the teacher may use the time and space released for something else.

> 2   *Successful teachers set the challenge and design learning processes to be neither too easy nor too difficult.* Digitalization in instruction does not mean making learning processes as easy (or even as difficult) as possible. What digitalization in instruction means is rather setting a level of difficulty that is adjusted to the prior knowledge of the learners and making learning as challenging as possible.
>
> 3   *Successful teachers see learning as hard work and integrate varied, regular, and challenging phases of practice into their lessons.* Digitalization in instruction does not mean shifting the learning exclusively into the hands of the learners. What digitalization in instruction means is rather opening up possibilities for deliberate learning.
>
> 4   *Successful teachers see instruction as interaction based on esteem and therefore make an effort to develop positive relationships.* Digitalization in instruction does not mean substituting social structures with new media and possibly even doing away with the teacher altogether. What digitalization in instruction means is rather using new media to integrate new forms of interaction, discussion, and cooperation into teaching and learning processes.
>
> 5   *Successful teachers see instruction not as a one-way street but as a dialogue.* Digitalization in instruction does not mean substituting the spoken word with digital exchange. What digitalization in instruction means is rather integrating prior and subsequent digital exchange to give the spoken word during the lesson a more profound and lasting effect.

Mindframes 2, 3, 4, and 5 can be summarized using the factor "Flipped Classroom." This method pursues exactly these goals (cf. Tan, Yue & Fu, 2017): The flipped classroom is an instructional strategy that provides a new methodology and modality for teaching and learning. It involves a role change for instructors as a way of minimizing the amount of direct instruction in their teaching practice while maximizing one-to-one interaction and more cooperative and collaborative contribution to the teaching process, which can improve and encourage social interaction, teamwork, and cultural diversity among students. The roles of students have a corresponding change from passive participants to active participants.

In their meta-analyses, Cui Tan, Wei-Gang Yue, and Yu Fu (2017) covered 29 studies (in nursery education) and came to the result that flipped classroom might help students improve in knowledge, skills, attitudes, self-learning, study satisfaction, critical thinking, and problem-solving skills. They reported over all aspects high effect sizes up to 1.13. What is the secret of flipped classroom and does flipped classroom work in every context?

Flipped classroom is a teaching method in which, above all through the use of new media, the teaching is literally turned upside down. In classical or traditional teaching, the development of a topic or material usually takes place in the classroom. Knowledge is taught in class—the majority of the lesson is used for input. The exercise phase often comes much too short and is shifted—also from the resulting lack of time—into exercises to be done at home. In the flipped classroom concept, videos or screencasts in particular, which can be used to develop a new theme, are given to the learners. They watch these videos at home and learn the new content. The input happens at the pace students want, when students want, and where students want. For example, when using videos, students can pause or rewind during the video. If questions or problems of understanding arise, the students can immediately ask the teacher via the internet or directly during the practice phases. This leaves time for exercises in the classroom. The teacher is not only a guide on the side, but a change agent as well and can provide individual support. They are responsible for the production, selection, and provision of suitable materials which are received by the students outside the class. In the exercise phase, questions that have arisen in the input phase can be taken up by the teacher. Input and practice phases are thus simply exchanged ("flipped") in space and time.

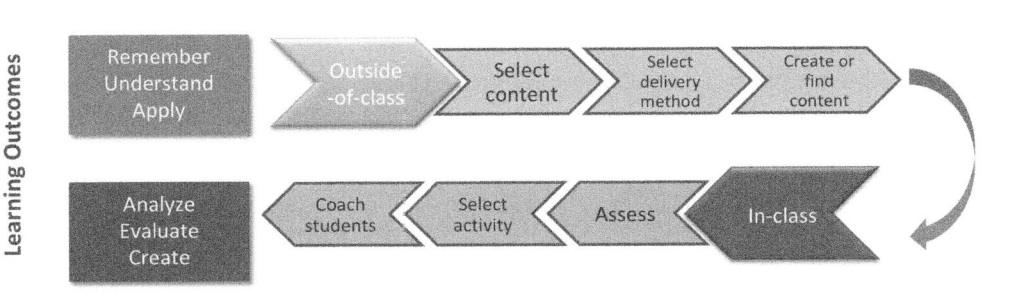

Figure 5.9 Flipped classroom

In the last years there have been numerous forms and developments of the flipped classroom concept. Possibilities, both in how and in which form the instruction is flipped, are already variously available, because there is no single strategy that works in every classroom, for every teacher and for each student (cf. Bergmann & Sams, 2014).

At the center of all considerations is the goal of establishing learner-centered teaching (instead of teacher-centered teaching) which takes into account and builds on the previous experiences, interests, and backgrounds of the learners. The method thus enables individualization and differentiation in the classroom, and the learners can be supported and challenged individually. This concept has drastically reduced the dropout rate at some learning locations.

It is quite possible to implement the flipped classroom with traditional media. In this way, input phases can be classically outsourced via books and worksheets. However, digital media once again offer the advantage that they make all this possible quickly and easily. Once again, it is the overcoming of space and time that creates the time and space for dialogue in the classroom.

Like any other method, the flipped classroom is subject to certain conditions. This includes, among other things:

a) The quality of the input that students should get for themselves outside the classroom is not unimportant. For example, there is a large number of explanation videos on YouTube on various topics. But not all of them are recommended. In this respect, it is particularly up to the teacher to make a suitable offer for the students. Please keep in mind that an explanation video has no possibility for interaction.

b) Due to the outsourcing of the input phase, the actual teaching receives more time and space for the deepening of what has been learned. This immediately shows that the outsourcing of the input phase is limited to a surface understanding and is not suitable for outsourcing deep understanding.

c) Learning in the flipped classroom requires more responsibility on the part of the students than traditional teaching. Students who do not prepare themselves thoroughly and who do not complete the input phases conscientiously cannot follow the attendance phase effectively. In this respect, a successful flipped classroom requires an intensive teacher–student relationship and effective teaching rules and rituals.

d) Students must have certain skills to learn in a flipped classroom. In addition to conscientiousness, this also includes the ability to practice self-assessment. Since the latter is not self-evident (keyword: Dunning-Kruger-Effect), the Flipped Classroom is to be introduced step by step depending on the performance level of the learners.

e) All this makes it clear: Flipped classroom is not just a technology at its core: It is an attitude to learning and teaching. As a result, it requires all participants to share a common vision of teaching that is often inconsistent with traditional patterns.

There is no doubt that for a flipped classroom to be successful, mindframes 2, 3, 4, and 5 are prerequisite.

> 6 *Successful teachers inform learners and parents about the language of education.* Digitalization in instruction does not mean lavishing unqualified praise on new media. What digitalization in instruction means is rather providing constructive criticism on the use of new media, pointing out its possibilities, limits, and dangers.

Digitalization is one of the most important issues for society as a whole and thus does not stop at families and children's rooms: Is a mobile phone harmful? At what age do children need a computer? How many hours of the internet are good for the child? These and many other questions concern parents—and also educational research. The discourse often fluctuates between euphoria and apocalypse. The truth, as so often, lies between extremes. So, what do we really know about digitalization and what recommendations can we make? First, the principle that technical progress brings opportunities, but also risks. Parents must weigh this up and decide according to the age and stage of development of the child. It will be important to make children and young people aware of the possibilities and limits of digitalization right from the start in order to lead them to a critical and constructive use of the media. This is the goal of education in the age of digitalization: People need to know when it pays to turn on digital media and when it is better to turn it off. For example, this is done by reflecting on television and internet consumption or analyzing communication via mobile phone in comparison to face-to-face interaction. Furthermore, it is advisable to agree on common rules of media consumption and to ensure that they are observed by all parties—including parents!—to pass the test. For example, no mobile phone use at the dining table or when driving a car or bicycle, no mobile phone transport in your trouser pockets or no long calls with a mobile phone without headphones, no internet times before going to bed, and much more. This also makes it clear to some parents that it would be better to play less with the mobile phone and pay more attention to the children (e.g., when breastfeeding!). And due to the increasing presence of digital media in a person's everyday life, conscious analogue times are worthwhile—walking together, playing together and even being bored together, which can be the origin of conversation, interaction, and creativity. All this is not because of a romantic longing for past times, but because we know from many studies that human beings need other human beings in order to recognize themselves, to grow, to self-develop. Machines do not turn human beings into human beings, but human beings need human beings. The challenge for schools is comprehensive media education, an education 4.0.

> 7 *Successful teachers see themselves as change agents and apply methods not for their own sake but always with an eye to the concrete learning situation.* Digitalization in

instruction does not mean applying new media because they are currently in vogue. What digitalization in instruction means is carefully considering the possibilities and needs of the learners and applying new media only and always when they are the best choice.

One of the most persistent arguments is that new media motivate students per se. At first glance, this is correct and it can be empirically proven that students learn in a more motivated manner when they receive a new tablet or a mobile phone, for example. At second glance, however, the same empirical studies also show that this motivation diminishes again after some time—at the latest when the students realize that it is all about learning. All this makes it clear: Learning needs motivation. For this to be sustainable, however, intrinsic rather than extrinsic motivation is needed. The ARCS model of John Keller can be helpful for this, as it almost combines evidence-based strategies of motivation. These can help teachers to critically question their choice of media with regard to the motivation of the students.

	Perceptual Arousal	**Inquiry Arousal**	**Variability**
Attention	Provide novelty and surprise	Stimulate curiosity by posing questions or problems to solve	Incorporate a range of methods and media to meet students' varying needs
	Goal Orientation	**Motive Matching**	**Familiarity**
Relevance	Present objectives and useful purpose of instruction and specific methods for successful achievement	Match objectives to student needs and motives	Present content in ways that are understandable and that are related to the learners' experiences and values
	Learning Requirements	**Successful Opportunities**	**Personal Responsibility**
Confidence	Inform students about learning and performance requirements and assessment criteria	Provide challenging and meaningful opportunities for successful learning	Link learning success to students' personal effort and ability
	Intrinsic Reinforcement	**Extrinsic Rewards**	**Equity**
Satisfaction	Encourage and support intrinsic enjoyment of the learning experience	Provide positive reinforcement and motivational feedback	Maintain consistent standards and consequences for success

Figure 5.10 ARCS model

8 *Successful teachers give and demand feedback, because they regard it not just as an important instrument but also as a basic dimension of instruction.* Digitalization in instruction does not mean doing away with all traditional forms of feedback and only seeking digital feedback. What digitalization in instruction means is rather reaping the additional benefits new media offer in comparison to traditional media and integrating feedback methods into the lesson that would otherwise not be possible on account of time constraints and a lack of competence.

9 *Successful teachers regard student achievements as feedback for themselves about themselves and always view the successes as well as the mistakes of their students in the learning process as connected to their own thinking and actions.* Digitalization in instruction does not mean letting technology take care of the exchange on mistakes in the learning process. What digitalization in instruction means is rather using new media to make mistakes in the learning process visible and then taking this as a basis for an intensive exchange about teaching and learning processes.

It is possible to combine mindframes 8 and 9 and explain both in more detail. Two points that can be crystallized out of the research on feedback are to be noted first: First, more important than the feedback we give is the feedback that reaches students. Second, the feedback from the students to the teacher is more important than the (classical) feedback from the teacher to the students. Especially in the latter case, digitalization offers new possibilities that do not only serve to bridge space and time. Take, for example, feedback from the students to the teacher with the help of an app (cf. Zierer & Wisniewski, 2018) during instruction or at the end of a lesson:

With the help of an app, the teacher can immediately see the result of the feedback and communicate directly with the students. If she or he uses a validated questionnaire, she or he can see what went well and what went badly in the classroom. Students can provide further feedback so that the dialogue on instruction, learning, and teaching is intensified and promoted. Figure 5.11 shows what the feedback of students with regard to the quality criterion "Captivate" looks like.

A teacher interviewed 9th grade students on six items about motivation:

(1) The requirement level of the lesson was appropriate for me.

(2) The pace of the lesson was appropriate for me.

(3) The teacher used the lesson time in such a way that I was able to make progress.

(4) The teacher has helped me to recognize connections myself.

(5) The contents of the lesson were taught by the teacher in an interesting way.

(6) The teacher varied different teaching methods.

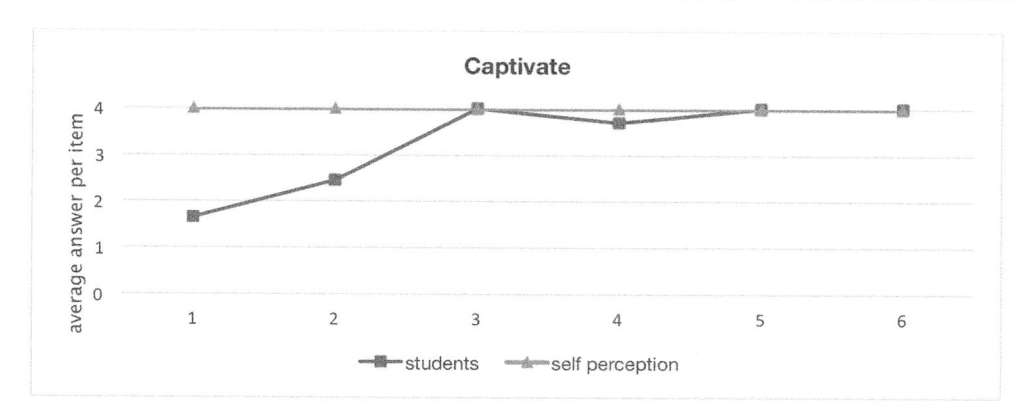

1: I don't agree • 2: I rather don't agree • 3: I rather agree • 4: I agree • 0: no answer

Figure 5.11 Feedback of students

As the chart in Figure 5.11 shows, the teacher perceived the degree of motivation in all areas as very high. For items three to six, the students largely agreed with this assessment. On the other hand, they rated items one and two less favorably than the teacher.

The feedback shows that a lot about motivation works very well in this class. The deviating perceptions of the first two items can be used as a basis for discussion.

• Why were the level of difficulty and pace of the lesson not appropriate for the learners?

• What measures can be taken to achieve a better fit?

Discussing the lesson on the basis of the collected behavioral data ensures that clear and verifiable change targets can be defined. The differentiated mapping of the "motivation" area using six empirically verified items also makes it possible to clearly identify the direction in which a possible change can take place.

Successful feedback depends on how it is communicated. If this is done well, it generates high satisfaction and acceptance in the feedback recipient and leads to an intention to change one's own behavior if necessary. From an empirical point of view, the following points can be demonstrated (cf. Kanning & Rustige, 2012): Satisfaction and acceptance depend to a large extent on the quality of the feedback, that is, on how substantively and comprehensibly it explains why something was perceived as positive or negative. If suggestions are made as to what should be changed, it is crucial to substantiate this argument soundly ("I am your teacher trainer," by the way, is not such a sound underpinning). Instead of "should have, could have, might have" feedback, a structured procedure including the following steps is therefore preferable:

a) comparison of the perspectives of the feedback recipient and the feedback provider with regard to concrete quality criteria;

b) thematization of the congruence and discrepancies between feedback and self-perception and the reasons for them;

c) joint consideration of possibilities for improvement based on the discrepancies;

d) agreement on goal(s).

But that's not all: The feedback a teacher has received from students using digital media allows her or him to exchange it quickly and easily with other teachers. Please think of a mentor at the school who was not present in class but should give feedback. Or even think of an expert in teaching, for example a researcher at a university, to whom you send the feedback you have received from the students. Both can look at the result at the time and place that suits them and give you feedback—by dialogue during a meeting, but also by e-mail, by video message, or by Skype. In these cases, the boundaries of time and space have moved very far behind. A prerequisite for this is that the teacher is supported by the mindframe to see feedback as a central building block of teacher professionalism.

10 *Successful teachers cooperate with each other.* Digitalization in instruction does not mean using new media to reduce the amount of exchange with other teachers or even replace it. What digitalization in instruction means is rather using new media to initiate new forms of exchange and cooperation between teachers.

There are without doubt many teachers who seek to exchange and cooperate with each other. It would thus be wrong to suggest that teachers do not work together with their colleagues at all. It is unfortunate, however, that this cooperation is not always put into actual practice everywhere and is largely neglected in teacher education programs, where it is not systematically required and fostered. More important, the focus of collaboration needs to be about the impact and effects on students. We need to share how we think and evaluate our impact much more than discuss curriculum, assessment tasks, and sharing engaging activities.

The importance and necessity of exchange and cooperation is often illustrated by means of biological comparisons: Ant and bee colonies are classic examples of how much benefit the individual can derive from the community and of how the whole can be greater than the sum of its parts. Although these two analogies do not work at every level—considering neither the greater diversity among humans nor the value of an open society—both describe an essential aspect of community in a democracy and, therefore, serve to illustrate a key message: Humans too can benefit from exchange and cooperation.

The factor "Micro-teaching" stands for a row of digital solutions which can improve cooperation. It refers to methods for planning small-scale lessons in a group and analyzing and discussing them with the help of videos. It can be expanded to viewing videos of teachers in their usual classrooms. This provides an under-the-microscope view of teaching practices and teaching behavior, but more important, it can allow discussion about the impact of teachers on the students. The effect size of 0.88 this factor achieves in *Visible Learning* (cf. Hattie & Zierer, 2017) testifies to its effectiveness. But we make a critical distinction between using micro-teaching to watch a teacher teach and to watch the impact of a teacher teaching. It is primarily the latter that makes the difference. It can also help to invite a teacher to "think aloud" as they watch themselves teach (especially when the audio is turned off) to hear their mindframes and the moment-by-moment decisions that they claim to have made. It is less the technology of "micro-teaching" but the opportunity to hear the thinking of teachers, to see their impact on students, and to create a common dialogue about thinking and impact.

The research findings demonstrate one thing clearly (cf. Hattie & Zierer, 2017): The necessary competence and attitude for successful cooperation, exchange, and collaboration need to be learned. Against this backdrop, a good place to start working on a mindframe for cooperation is to first become conscious of your own behavior about exchange and cooperation and then use this knowledge to identify the fields in which more cooperation can have a lasting positive effect. The following list can be useful for this reflection. It attempts to identify various levels of cooperation and arrange them in order of difficulty:

Steps of cooperation

1   Discussing with one another
2   Supporting and criticizing one other
3   Planning and evaluating lessons together
4   Delivering lessons together.

This sequence of steps shows that working together does not essentially mean exchanging learning and teaching materials, first and foremost worksheets ... Too often cooperation at this level is atrophied. Instead, this list is based on a deeper understanding of cooperation: planning, implementing, and evaluating together. Therefore it is easier to discuss general criteria of instruction than to support and criticize one another's concrete ideas for a lesson, and both steps are easier than planning and evaluating lessons together. The crowning point of cooperation between teachers is then delivering lessons together and evaluating the impact of these lessons on students together—particularly as this represents the consummation of all the teamwork and therefore involves bringing together not just the thinking but also the action of the team members.

The core skill is working together on what are agreed success criteria, what is the current diagnosis of what the students know and are able to do, and whether the planned intervention is highly likely to move the students from where they are to where we all want them to be. It is this joint discussion about appropriate criteria of success and the expected levels of growth over the course of the lessons that matters the most.

New media give teachers the opportunity to work on joint planning, implementation, and evaluation processes independent of time and space. In view of the complexity of school and teaching, the density of appointments and obligations that every teacher has to cope with day in, day out, there is great potential. In this sense, school is not only a place for learning 4.0 and education 4.0, but also a place for work 4.0.

Teachers who succeed in entering the classroom equipped with these mindframes will integrate digitalization into their instruction in a meaningful way. This does not mean we have to hate the internet (2016), as Jarett Kobek claims he does in the title of his new book, nor does it mean we have to praise it. It is a medium, and it will always be a medium. It needs human beings to breathe life into it.

Summary

WHAT MAKES UP TEACHER PROFESSIONALIZATION, AND WHAT CONSEQUENCES DOES IT HAVE FOR DIGITALIZATION IN EDUCATION?

At the core of teacher professionalization is the interplay between competence and mindframes with regard to the subject, the pedagogy, and the didactics. What this implies for digitalization in education is that possibilities and limits, success and failure, should not depend solely on the ability and knowledge of the teachers but also and especially on their will and judgment. This leads to the challenge of not just creating the structures for digitalization but always also strengthening the people.

WHY IS THE FACTOR "OUTDOOR/ADVENTURE PROGRAMS" SO EFFECTIVE, AND WHAT CONCLUSIONS DOES THIS SUGGEST FOR LEARNING 4.0?

Outdoor and adventure programs achieve a large effect size and are characterized by follow-up effects, meaning that their positive effect is measurable even in the long term. The main reasons for this effectiveness are challenging goals, intensive cooperation, and trusting relationships. It is therefore less the method that produces the effects of such programs than the interpersonal interaction they initiate and support.

WHY IS FOCUSING ON HUMAN BEINGS THE MOST IMPORTANT FACTOR OF SUCCESSFUL DIGITAL LEARNING?

The main message across all theories and empirical studies is that technology alone will not revolutionize instruction. Instead, it is always the people who decide whether digitalization has a positive effect. The danger of reversing this principle is also backed up by theory and empirical data: Putting technology before pedagogy can mean failing to consider the question of why and regarding the human being as a means to an end. However, education always takes the human being as its starting point and places human beings at the center of pedagogical thinking and action.

6

Conclusion

Pedagogy before technology

Task for reflection

Reflect on how the ideas discussed in this book have changed your understanding of digitalization in education and learning: Where are the possibilities and where are the limits of digitalization? Who bears responsibility for education and learning? What can each of us do to improve the world through digitalization?

Goals

This chapter attempts to sum up the main messages of this book. This summary is guided by the principle of putting pedagogy before technology. When you finish reading this chapter, you should be able to answer the following questions:

* What is meant by the grammar of learning and why is it so important in the context of digitalization?
* What are the next steps for each school to master digitalization?
* What is meant by the principle "pedagogy before technology"?

Digitalization changes everything: A mantra that is often said these days. It may be true for certain contexts, such as the world of work, industry, and education, but it is not only inadequate, it is even dangerous. For this mantra ignores the fact that human evolution is not the same as technical innovation. The grammar of learning that has emerged with the development of *Homo sapiens* illustrates this misconception—and this is exemplified by five principles that emerge above all in the course of the digitalization of schools.

The grammar of learning

First, learning requires effort and commitment: The current thesis is that learning through digitalization changes completely. It can be refuted by a central grammar of learning, which can be illustrated by means of the forgetting curve. For example, we know from numerous psychological studies that a person needs about six to eight repetitions in order to transfer information from short-term memory into long-term memory. If these repetitions and the associated effort and the necessary commitment are lacking, forgetting takes its course. So the moment of forgetting begins at the moment of remembering. And this is independent of whether analog or digital learning has taken place.

Second, learning requires challenges: It is one of the most consistent messages from technology companies that digitalization makes learning easier. As beautiful as this thesis sounds, as wrong it is: Education in general and learning in particular is not easy because it progresses by detours and wrong paths, often leads to failure and mistakes, and generates errors. In this respect, education must not be about making learning as easy as possible. It must be about making learning as challenging as possible. The flow experience is the best empirical proof of this grammar of learning: People reach the state of deep satisfaction when they pursue a task that challenges them and insofar as the probability of success is as great as the probability of failure. If digitalization is to be effective in education, it must be used in such a way that the challenge can be set even better without it.

Third, learning requires positive relationships: One of the central results of anthropology is that human beings need counterparts to recognize themselves. In Martin Buber's work, it is accordingly said: A person becomes an I through a You. If the other person is missing, one feels like Robinson Crusoe—one becomes lonely and abandoned and loses oneself in a world without support and orientation. This insight can now be empirically proven several times, for example with the Dunning-Kruger effect: People tend to overestimate or underestimate their possibilities. Only rarely does the picture you draw of yourself hit the mark. The external assessment is important in order to rub against it and to question oneself. In this respect, the talk—fueled by digitalization—of the learning guide and excessive individualized learning is not very helpful either, but rather absurd. Learners do not only need a "guide on the side." They also need a "change agent" at every stage of their lives, as *Visible Learning* makes clear—a person who holds up a mirror to students, encourages them, and sets them the challenge if they do not believe in themselves, but also slows them down if they have false expectations of themselves. The grammar of learning therefore includes teachers who act with a conscious and responsible willingness to change—well aware that they can only offer learning situations that the learner can only use herself or himself.

Fourth, learning requires motivation: The classic discussion about the benefits of digitalization in education is the thesis that the use of tablets, mobile phones, etc. increases the motivation to learn. This can be empirically portrayed beautifully and confirmed at first glance. At second glance, however, it becomes apparent that this increase in motivation decreases again after two to four weeks—at the latest when learners realize that it is still all about learning. And so this digitalization argument suffers from the ignorance of the grammar of learning that learning requires motivation. But in essence and in the long run, it is not motivation that lies outside of learning, but motivation that is focused on the thing that needs to be learned. It is not extrinsic motivation that is the key to success; it is intrinsic motivation.

Fifth, learning requires surface understanding in order to develop deep understanding: In times of Alexa and Siri it may be indisputable for many that thanks to digitalization people no longer need factual knowledge. Against this background, the argument is: Knowledge is available anytime and anywhere so that learners can fully concentrate on self-development, transfer and problem solving, and creativity. This reasoning ignores the difference between factual knowledge and wisdom as well as the connection between surface understanding and deep understanding, as it has always been known in instruction, teaching, and learning sciences. In order for learners to enter the realm of deep understanding, which is the goal of education as meaningful, creative, and problem-solving thinking, they must have acquired a certain degree of factual knowledge. Just knowing where something stands and where information can be found is not enough. Deep understanding is based on surface understanding. And for learners to be able to process it further, the facts must be in their minds—and not on hard disks and memory cards.

Many more such principles of learning could be mentioned, but the core message is already visible: As long as we human beings are human beings, learning remains learning. Digitalization will not change that. And everyone who claims and pushes this is mistaking human beings and making machines out of human beings. For many it may well be a goal to replace *Homo sapiens* with *Homo digitales* or at least to "upgrade" it—according to the motto: Artificial intelligence is the solution for human stupidity. But then we will no longer talk about education, but programming. And it no longer counts what I have made of my life, but what they have made of me. But if we continue to talk about human beings and their education, then it is worth paying attention to the grammar of learning.

The next steps for each school

Digitalization is a part of our lives today more than ever before. A school that shuts itself off from the educational tasks this reality requires would fail to fulfill its educational mission. However, this mission always also involves pointing out possibilities and limitations and making decisions for the good of the children and youths. Digitalization for the sake of digitalization runs counter to this good, because it blindly follows the dictates of technology and loses sight of human beings, their needs, and their possibilities in the process. To put it in more concise terms: Children do not only need to learn to turn on new media. They also need to learn when it is time to turn it off again. And the same thing goes for teachers and their instruction: Teachers need to know when it is worth it to integrate new media into their lessons and when it is better to work with traditional media. This results in various fields of development for making digital learning successful. Four of these fields are described in more detail in the following.

The first field of development is "educational expertise": It is clear from the use of new media in pedagogical contexts that success is not contingent only on the knowledge and ability of the teachers. Pronounced subject matter competence is not sufficient, nor is a high level of pedagogical and didactic competence. Rather, all of this knowledge and ability needs to be accompanied by will and judgment. Competence (in the form of knowledge and ability) and mind frames (in the form of will and judgment) are hence crucial for the success of pedagogical interventions, and they appear from an epistemological standpoint as two sides of the same coin (cf. Zierer, 2015b). So how can teachers be brought to combine competence and mind frames in handling and applying new media?

The second field of development is a "culture of mistakes": New media are always a connecting link between the learner and the teacher. They therefore serve as a means to an end within this interaction. They can foster learning, but they can also hinder learning. Research on new media already shows today that much will depend on the existence of a learning culture that welcomes mistakes or even shifts them to the center of the interaction. The example of the physical education teacher presented above may again serve as an illustration: If this teacher makes a digital recording of a learner's movement patterns and watches it with her backwards and forwards and in slow motion, then the teacher is using new media to look for mistakes, to understand mistakes as a learning opportunity, to make mistakes the focus of teaching (cf. Hattie & Zierer, 2017). This way of dealing with mistakes should not be taken for granted. New media can help to establish such a culture of mistakes. Doing so involves answering the following questions: What conditions must the learners and the teacher meet and what features must new media have to foster such a culture of mistakes?

The third field of development is a "culture of cooperation": One of the areas with the greatest potential for enhancing performance in pedagogical contexts is that of exchange and cooperation between teachers. This is indicated both by general studies, such as *The Rational Optimist* by Matt Ridley (2010), and by empirical studies such as the works by John Hattie discussed above (2013, 2014; with Yates, 2015; with Zierer, 2017). The keyword in this context is "collective intelligence." New media offer a wide range of possibilities for exchange and cooperation, although they will not come about of their own accord. What we need to ask is therefore how to design new media and integrate them into the process of exchange and cooperation in such a way that they facilitate the development of collective intelligence and make it visible, exerting in this way a positive influence on the professionalism of teachers.

The fourth field of development is "evidence basis": The flood of programs and games, apps, and the like we are confronted with today demands more than ever an evidence-based orientation in research and practice. Success is not just a matter of using new media but of using them to foster stable learning processes. This results in the challenge of elucidating when and especially why certain new media are successful in supporting educational processes, when and why this is not the case, and how teachers can succeed in answering these questions in the classroom. And this brings us back to the first field of development, "educational expertise": Teachers need the necessary competence and mind frames for working with new media but also with regard to their own professionalism. Seeing oneself as responsible for the education of learners and scrutinizing one's own behavior on this point is one of the most important qualities of successful teachers (cf. Hattie & Zierer, 2017).

It is therefore up to us as teachers to determine what future we are aiming at. I have often used the pictures shown in Figures 6.1 and 6.2 in the past to illustrate the potential extremes.

Figure 6.1 Digital future

Source: peshkova, fotolia.com

Figure 6.2 Humanity

Source: Joss, fotolia.com

Technically possible vs. pedagogically sensible

What do we want? Why is digitalization in education important for us? In answering these questions, it is useful in my mind to draw a distinction first between what is *technically possible* and what is *pedagogically sensible* and second between what follows for *learning* and what should be borne in mind for *education*.

It is already technically possible today to use a face scan to obtain information on the emotional state of learners, but is it pedagogically sensible to do so? If teachers need to consult this information one day, then it will probably already be too late. In a pedagogical atmosphere, learners approach teachers when they have problems, and teachers address learners when they notice that something is wrong. It is already technically possible today to package learning processes in such a way that children and youths do not even realize that they are learning, but is it pedagogically sensible to do so? If we interpret learning as entertainment, we fail to appreciate the significance of learning for education and ignore the grammar of learning, which involves challenges, effort, and hard work as well as detours, wrong turns, and mistakes. It is already technically possible today to get along without learning foreign languages, because a computer can serve as a simultaneous interpreter, but is it pedagogically sensible to do so? Foreign languages are more than words. They are bearers of culture, of values and norms, of history. Not without good reason did Johann Wolfgang von Goethe conclude that people who do not know foreign languages know nothing of their own. It is already technically possible today to have a laptop computer give the learner a signal when it is time to take a break, but is it pedagogically sensible to do so? The goal of education can be seen as forming responsible citizens who are free of constraints and capable of making decisions on the basis of their own sense of reason. Education thus consists not in what *someone else* made out of me but what *I myself* made out of my own life.

Technology must be made to serve people, not the other way around. When technology robs people of their freedom and their responsibility, then people will become machines—and we will find ourselves in the situation about which (maybe) Albert Einstein says: "I fear the day that technology will surpass our human interaction. The world will have a generation of idiots." And so it is that the question of the possibilities of digitalization is always connected with the limitations of digitalization and always necessitates weighing the opportunities for learning against the risks for education. A comprehensive media education—consisting of media knowledge, media use, media production, and media criticism—is hence the fundamental task of digitalization in education.

Thinking about post-digitalization

The post-growth economy is a scientific and socio-political positioning that radically questions what goes without saying. In the focus above all is the three-step economy–growth–prosperity. What's wrong with that? For many, it is the guarantor of human success, human health, and human wellbeing. With all the approval that this success deserves, because it is easy to make visible with statistics, there is justified doubt about whether this success is not just one side of the coin. If one follows the three perspectives—economic, ecological, and social—of the post-growth economy, it can be stated: Never before has the gap between rich and poor in this world been so wide. Never before have so many people been on the run—because of hunger, war, displacement. Never before has global warming increased so much. Never before have so many people worldwide lost themselves in loneliness. Never before have so many insects died, so much waste landed in the oceans, so many areas deserted, so much earth contaminated with radioactivity, and so much air and light been polluted. And never before have the global markets been so competitive and tense.

Despite all optimism à la Hans Rosling (2018) in *Factfullness*, the world is not only in balance: The world has also fallen apart. There is no doubt that it is worth thinking differently, taking off the rose-tinted glasses and questioning what seems to be taken for granted and to regard it as something that cannot be taken for granted. Ultimately, this is associated with an age-old, ancient claim to human judgment: Every value has an equivalent value. And the truth so often lies between extremes. So where is the right level, the golden middle?

Currently, this claim seems to have fallen into oblivion, especially if you look at the positions on the permanent topic: Digitalization is the key word and for many a driving force for innovation, a guarantor of prosperity, the crystallization point of the next revolution—only unfortunately revolutions are not always good for people. If one takes the perspectives of the post-growth economy, it can already be seen today that digitalization has a dark side that must not be lost sight of.

From an economic perspective, digitalization will undoubtedly open up new markets. Due to the pace of progress, these will be more controversial and unclear than ever before—technical developments used to extend over generations, but today they will take place in just a few months, sometimes even weeks. The resulting markets will also have dramatic effects on the world of work: Many jobs will certainly be lost because digitalization makes them superfluous—robotics and artificial intelligence are the magic words. The mantra of many corporations that new jobs are certainly being created may be true, but it remains vague to this day. The only thing that seems safe is that new jobs will require new skills for which the majority of society is not prepared and cannot be prepared quickly. The economy will change as a result of digitalization—both positive and negative.

From a social perspective, the consequences of digitalization can already be better assessed. One example: 99 percent of the next generation has a mobile phone and uses it about 240 minutes a day. For many young people, the mobile phone is more important than friendship, although many complain of stress resulting from unthinking mobile phone use. Addictive design is the key word in this context and it makes the following point clear: Digitalization does not only have positive effects on human beings.

And finally, the consequences of digitalization are already visible today from an ecological perspective: modern technology is based on rare-earth metals that can only be extracted under the most difficult conditions and with the greatest of effort. Moreover, these resources are limited and will one day come to an end—the disposal of the electronic waste of industrialized countries in poorer countries does the rest. As a result, every mobile phone is anything but sustainable, leaving an ecologically problematic footprint. And by the way: The Robo-Bee will not solve the problem of insect death.

It is therefore worth questioning digitalization and already today thinking about its possibilities, but also about its limits. The age of digitalization will be followed by the age of post-digitalization. The responsibility of the older generation for the next generation requires concern and criticism. So it is not only a question of whether the glass is half full or half empty. Both perspectives are important and help to find the right measure, the golden middle.

Put pedagogy before technology

There is no doubt in my mind that the arguments presented in this book and the empirical findings on digital learning suggest the following conclusion:

Digitalization is an important element in making schools fit for the future, but it is not a magic formula for mastering all pedagogical challenges. The place of education in teaching and learning processes should be seen as lying in human encounters. School education remains essentially a question of successful interaction between people. Technology should be integrated into this interaction in a meaningful way and subordinated to human considerations. In a word: Put pedagogy before technology!

Summary

WHAT IS MEANT BY THE GRAMMAR OF LEARNING AND WHY IS IT SO IMPORTANT IN THE CONTEXT OF DIGITALIZATION?

Learning is and will remain learning. It is essentially subject to evolutionary aspects and not to technical developments. This can be seen in a number of principles that clarify the grammar of learning.

WHAT ARE THE NEXT STEPS FOR EACH SCHOOL TO MASTER DIGITALIZATION?

Schools must continue to develop if they want to master the digital transformation. Four fields of development seem indispensable for this: educational expertise; culture of mistakes; culture of cooperation; evidence basis.

WHAT IS MEANT BY THE PRINCIPLE "PEDAGOGY BEFORE TECHNOLOGY"?

The main message across all theories and empirical studies is that technology alone will not revolutionize instruction. Instead, it is always the people who decide whether digitalization has a positive effect. The danger of reversing this principle is also backed up by theory and empirical data: Putting technology before pedagogy can mean failing to consider the question of why and regarding the human being as a means to an end. However, education always takes the human being as its starting point and places human beings at the center of pedagogical thinking and action. And against this background it is worthwhile thinking about post-digitalization.

References

Baacke, D. (1997). *Medienpädagogik*. Tübingen: Niemeyer.

Baumert, J., & Kunter, M. (2006). Stichwort: Professionelle Kompetenz von Lehrkräften. In: *Zeitschrift für Erziehungswissenschaft, 9,* 469–520.

Bergmann, J., & Sams, A. (2014). *Flipped learning*. London: ISTE.

Biggs, J., & Collis, K. (1982). *Evaluating the quality of learning: The SOLO taxonomy*. New York: Academic Press.

Birkelbach, R., et al. (Eds.). (2001). *Guinness Buch der Rekorde*. Hamburg: Guinness.

Blömeke, S., Kaiser, G., & Lehmann, R. (Eds.) (2010). *TEDS-M 2008: Professionelle Kompetenz und Lerngelegenheiten angehender Primarstufenlehrkräfte im internationalen Ver- gleich*. Münster: Waxmann.

Bloom, B. (1984). *Taxonomy of educational objectives* (1956). New York: Pearson Education.

Brezinka, W. (1990). *Grundbegriffe der Erziehungswissenschaft – Analyse, Kritik, Vorschläge*. 5th edition. München: Reinhardt.

Bundesministerium für Familie, Senioren, Frauen und Jugend (2017). *Bericht über die Lebenssituation junger Menschen und die Leistungen der Kinder- und Jugendhilfe in Deutschland*. Berlin: Federal Republic of Germany.

Carr, N. G. (2010). *The shallows: What the internet is doing to our brains*. New York: Norton.

Chandler, P., & Sweller, J. (1991). Cognitive load theory and the format of instruction. *Cognition and Instruction, 8,* 293–332.

Common Sense (2017). www.commonsensemedia.org/videos/introduction-to-the-samr-model (last accessed 04/27/2017).

Fend, H. (2006). *Neue Theorie der Schule. Einführung in das Verstehen von Bildungssystemen*. Wiesbaden: VS.

Flechsig, K.-H. (1991). *Kleines Handbuch didaktischer Modelle*. Nörten-Hardenberg: Zentrum für didaktische Studien e.V.

Gardner, H. (2013): *Intelligenzen*. Stuttgart: Klett-Cotta.

Gardner, H., Csíkszentmihályi, M., & Damon, W. (2005). *Good Work. Für eine neue Ethik im Beruf*. Stuttgart: Klett-Cotta.

German Council of Education (Ed.) (1970). *Strukturplan für das Bildungswesen*. Stuttgart: Klett.

Hattie, J. (2013). *Lernen sichtbar machen*. Baltmannsweiler: Schneider.

Hattie, J. (2014). *Lernen sichtbar machen für Lehrpersonen*. Baltmannsweiler: Schneider.

Hattie, J., & Yates, G. C. R. (2015). *Lernen sichtbar machen aus psychologischer Perspektive*. Baltmannsweiler: Schneider.

Hattie, J., & Zierer, K. (2017). *10 mindframes for visible learning*. London: Routledge.

Heidegger, M. (1954). *Die Frage nach der Technik*. Stuttgart: Neske.

Kanning, U. P., & Rustige, J. (2012). Der Stellenwert von Feedback-Regeln aus empirischer Sicht. *Personalführung, 5/2012,* 24–31.

Kearney, M., Schuck, S., Burden, K., & Aubusson, P. (2012). Viewing mobile learning from a pedagogical perspective. *Research in Learning Technology*, 20: 14406. doi:10.3402/rlt.v20i0/14406

Klafki, W. (1996). *Neue Studien zur Bildungstheorie und Didaktik. Zeitgemäße Allgemeinbildung und kritisch-konstruktive Didaktik.* 5th edition. Weinheim: Beltz.

Kobek, J. (2016). *Ich hasse dieses Internet.* Frankfurt am Main: Fischer.

Koehler, M. J., & Mishra, P. (2009). What is technological pedagogical content knowledge? *Contemporary Issues in Technology and Teacher Education*, 9(1), 60–70.

Kunter, M., Baumert, J., Blum, W., Klusmann, U., Krauss, S., & Neubrand, M. (Eds.) (2011). *Professionelle Kompetenz von Lehrkräften. Ergebnisse des Forschungsprogramms COACTIV.* Münster: Waxmann.

Mishra, P., & Koehler, M. J. (2006). Technological pedagogical content knowledge: A framework for teacher knowledge. *Teachers College Record*, 108(6), 1017–1054. doi:10.1111/j.1467-9620.2006.00684.x.

Mobilelearningtoolkit (2018). www.mobilelearningtoolkit.com/ipac-framework.html (last accessed 07/17/2018).

Montag, Chr. (2018). *Homo digitales.* Wiesbaden: Springer.

Moritz, H. (2011). *Elektrosmog: Ursachen, Gesundheitsrisiken, Schutzmaßnahmen.* Aachen: Shaker.

Mueller, P. A., & Oppenheimer, D. M. (2014). The pen is mightier than the keyboard. *Psychological Science*, 25(6), 1159–1168.

Mutter, J. (2013). *Lass dich nicht vergiften! Warum Schadstoffe chronisch krank machen und wie wir ihnen entkommen.* München: Gräfe und Unzer.

Pant, H. A., Stanat, P., Schroeders, U., Roppelt, A., Siegle, T., & Pöhlmann, C. (2013). *IQB-Ländervergleich 2012.* Münster: Waxmann.

Postman, N. (1985). *Amusing ourselves to death: Public discourse in the age of show business.* New York: Penguin Books.

Prensky, M. (2010). *Teaching digital natives. Partnering for real learning.* Thousand Oaks, California: Corwin Press.

Prenzel, M., Sälzer, Chr., Klieme, E., & Köller, O. (2014): *PISA 2012. Fortschritte und Herausforderungen in Deutschland.* Münster: Waxmann.

Puentedura, R. C. (2017a). http://hippasus.com/resources/sweden2010/SAMR_TPCK_Intro ToAdvancedPractice.pdf (last accessed 04/27/2017).

Puentedura, R. C. (2017b). www.youtube.com/watch?v=W6j8soDYoaw&feature=youtu.be (last accessed 04/27/2017).

Ridley, M. (2010). *The Rational Optimist.* New York: Harper.

Rosling, H. (2018). *Factfulness.* New York: Flatiron.

Shulman, L. S. (1986). Those who understand: Knowledge growth in teaching. *Educational Researcher*, 15(2), 4–14.

Sinek, S. (2016). Millenials. www.youtube.com/watch?v=NEsUudZvntE (last accessed 07/20/2018).

Spitzer, M. (2014). *Digitale Demenz. Wie wir uns und unsere Kinder um den Verstand bringen.* München: Droemer.

Spivack, N. (2017). www.novaspivack.com (last accessed 05/09/2017).

Stetina, B. U., & Kryspin-Exner, I. (Eds.) (2009). *Gesundheit und Neue Medien. Psychologische Aspekte der Interaktion mit Informations- und Kommunikationstechnologien.* Vienna: Springer.

Tan, C., Yue W.-G., & Fu, Y. (2017). Effectiveness of flipped classrooms in nursing education: Systematic review and meta-analysis. *Chinese Nursing Research*, 4(4), 192–200.

Ward, A. F., Duke, K., Gneezy, A., & Bos, M. W. (2017). Brain drain: The mere presence of one's own smartphone reduces available cognitive capacity. *Journal of the Association for Consumer Research*, 2(2), 140–154.

We Are Social & Hootsuite (2018). Global digital report 2018. https://wearesocial.com/blog/2018/01/global-digital-report-2018 (last accessed 07/19/2018).

Webb, N. (1997). *Research monograph number 6: Criteria for alignment of expectations and assessments on mathematics and science education.* Washington, D.C.: CCSSO.

Weber, E. (1999). *Pädagogik – Eine Einführung.* Vol. I, Part 3. Donauwörth: Auer.

Wheeler, S. (2017). www.steve-wheeler.co.uk/2010/07/web-x0-and-beyond.html (last accessed 05/09/2017).

Wilke, A. (2017). http://homepages.uni-paderborn.de/wilke/blog/2016/01/06/SAMR-Puentedura-deutsch/ (last accessed 04/27/2017).

Wolf, M. (2007). *Proust and the squid. The story and science of the reading brain.* New York: Harper.

Zierer, K. (2014). *Hattie für gestresste Lehrer.* Baltmannsweiler: Schneider.

Zierer, K. (2015a). *Conditio Humana.* 4. Auflage. Baltmannsweiler: Schneider.

Zierer, K. (2015b). Educational expertise. The concept of 'mind frames' as an integrative model for professionalisation in teaching. *Oxford Review of Education*, 41(6), 782–798.

Zierer, K., & Wisniewski, B. (2018): *Using student feedback for successful teaching.* London: Routledge.

Index of image sources

Index